M000091997

50

Marketing Secrets
of Growth Companies
in Down Economic Times

A Small Business Owner's Guide to
Surviving & Thriving in a Recession

By Sherré DeMao

GREENCASTLE
publishing

GreenCastle Publishing
137 Cross Center Road, Suite 239, Denver, NC 28037
www.greencastlepublishing.com
704.483.7283

Credits:
Cover Design, Sharon Bunting
Editor, Bea Quirk
Assistant Editor, Jessica Sumney
Indexer, Wendy Allex

© 2010 Sherré DeMao. All rights reserved.

Library of Congress Control Number: 2010908185

ISBN 978-0-9841051-1-3

Printed in the United States of America

For rights or permissions inquiries, please contact
GreenCastle Publishing at info@greencastlepublishing.com

For information about special quantity sales, premium or corporate packages,
please contact SLD Unlimited Marketing/PR, Inc. at 704.483.2941 or
sales@greencastlepublishing.com

Dedicated to:

U.S. Small Business Development Centers,
North Carolina Small Business Center Network,
and the thousands of small business owners I have met
over the years who inspired me to do the CRISP research
and to continually answer their questions about
"How Do I Market My Small Business?"

Donna,

Put these secrets
and the CRISP Principle
to work for you and watch
your business prosper like
never before!

Sherré
8.24.10

Table of Contents

Introduction

After more than 25 years working with small businesses, I have witnessed time and time again the frustration business owners feel as they continually seek the best ways to market their business for the greatest return. While there is great knowledge when it comes to their products, services and capabilities, confidence wanes when it comes to promoting the business in the marketplace.

When I started my company as a graphic design firm in 1984, I was dealing with the same challenge. I attended a graphics arts school, so there were no marketing, business or public relations classes for me to take. I didn't even know where to begin. However, as a freelance graphic designer and creative copywriter, I was expected to be knowledgeable about marketing as I created logos, brochures and other promotional materials for my clients.

Always loving a challenge, I went back to school, taking courses in marketing, business, psychology, and communications — anything and everything that would help me know more and become a better resource to my growing client base. My clients went back to school with me. They anxiously wanted to learn what I had learned, literally asking me to share my assignments as we worked on their graphics projects. It didn't take me long to realize what my own personal mission as a business owner should be: helping other business owners become savvier, more confident marketers.

By 1990, my purpose continued to prove a worthy one as my graphics company evolved into a full-service marketing firm. It was exciting and exhilarating. I also began to teach marketing to small businesses through the Senior Corps of Retired Executives Small Business Administration programs, as well as through Corporate & Continuing Education offerings at area colleges. It was just another way I felt I could fulfill my mission. So many businesses have a hunger to understand how to more effectively market their businesses, but lack the budget to hire an outside firm to assist them.

If you are in a business start-up or planning to start a business, I congratulate you for wanting to do it right. This book was developed to help you avoid the mistakes I have seen so many owners make when they market their businesses.

If you have been in business for years, I guarantee you will learn new ways to approach your marketing, enabling you to implement some tactics you have not used in your business.

What makes the information in this book so powerful is the fact that it is based on what truly works. It will help you make better and more productive marketing decisions for your business. This book is taking my mission to create savvier marketers to its ultimate level. This, my fellow business owners, is incredibly gratifying!

CRISP Principle: The Study

As a marketing consultant and instructor for small business marketing classes, I often hear the same questions from owners: "How do I market my small business?" "Where is my money best spent?" "Why hasn't what I have been doing worked?" "Where do I begin?"

After about 10 years in business, my marketing services firm adopted and perfected an approach that realized great success for our clients. The problem was, it was just our approach. I wanted something more than "this is the way we recommend doing it." I wanted validity. I wanted confirmation. I wanted something that qualified, quantified and verified what worked and what didn't work. I became more and more convinced that the marketing industry needed to do a better job at providing businesses with concrete initiatives that could be measured and confirmed.

In 1999, I decided to start tracking successful companies outside our client base to gauge what they were doing from a marketing standpoint. I specifically looked at companies that were successful and pretty much doing it on their own. My reasons were two-fold. First, I wanted to validate that the approach we were recommending to clients was not just something we had come up with, but was a time-tested approach being used by a number of successful firms. Second, I wanted to gain as much additional insight as I possibly could in my continuous mission to help business owners become savvier marketers and managers of their businesses.

Notice how I said "validate" rather than "prove"? This is a vital distinction. Anyone in market research knows you can prove anything you want. It is all a matter of how you ask the questions. However, validation means that there is the possibility the theory could be proven wrong or your research will have a different outcome than expected. Therefore, I spent about 18 months developing the survey and testing it to make sure I had covered all the bases, not just from a marketing perspective, but also from an operational one. This was significant because I believed businesses needed to view marketing as an integral part of operations, not as a separate function.

By late 2002, I was ready to send out the survey. It covered both sides of six legal-sized pages. Given that the survey was sent to busy business owners and that the typical response rate for such surveys is two percent, I was prepared to do several mailings to get enough responses to begin tabulations and analysis. Many told me I was crazy to think business owners would complete the survey because they already had enough demands on them.

Well, it turned out I was crazy like a fox. I received a 27 percent response from the first mailing. I believe there were two critical success factors. One, it was a blind survey returned in a pre-paid business reply envelope so participants could remain anonymous while sharing critical financial information. Second, I promised to send the survey results to those who participated. This was the real value to the business owners who participated. It was accomplished by having them send a completely separate request on a pre-paid postage reply card asking to see the results when they were released. Those who were already successful participated because they wanted to see if there was anything else they could or should be doing. Those who were frustrated by and not seeing the results they hoped for were anxious to learn what they could be doing differently.

I knew I had embarked on a much needed initiative when businesses called into our office requesting another survey to use as a checklist to base their strategy on in the future. Just by taking the survey, many business owners realized there were critical areas of their business they had not been considering. This made me even more excited and impassioned about my mission.

We continued to seek participation in the survey through the end of 2003, and then released the findings in 2004. Much to my delight, the approach we were recommending, now known as The CRISP Principle: Power of Five® was validated. The CRISP Principle: Power of Five® is based on the five tactics EVERY business should use for maximum success in its marketing strategy. These tactics should be the foundational core of every business marketing program. They are as follows:

1. The POWER of customer relations
2. The POWER of referral relations
3. The POWER of an Internet presence
4. The POWER of strategic involvements
5. The POWER of public relations

Out of this research came an astounding correlation between a company's growth and the number of CRISP Principles employed, both strategically and operationally. This finding was of special interest because the study looked at companies that grew in spite of the aftermath of 9-11 and the economic downturn of 2002-2003. Companies that did not grow only put a couple of the principles into play and on a superficial level at best. There was no clear strategy associated with what was being done. The result was wasted marketing dollars and chalking it up to the economy. Does this sound like you?

We also sought in our research to comprehensively validate image approaches, operational practices and attitudes that were dominant in growth companies. You will see the results of this segment of our research in the Image & Attitudes portion of this book.

When you have finished reading this book, you will market your business in a more effective way. You will implement tactics your competitors are not. Marketing will no longer be a mystery. It will be fun and rewarding. Doesn't that sound more like it?

IMAGE
&
ATTITUDES

1
Brand Image

A company's image is what captures the attention of prospective customers or steers them in a different direction. A company's image can make lasting positive impressions or create confusion and misperceptions. High-growth companies know how to effectively manage and present their image as a brand. If you accomplish this, you will have a distinctive image because you have established strong brand awareness and a perception of your company that people can embrace and appreciate. With this comes loyalty and preference of your business over competitors. Are you effectively and consistently branding your company in the following four image areas?

Physical Image: This applies to your business location as well as how you, your team and those associated with your business present themselves. Does your business have curb appeal? When someone pulls into your parking lot or sees the exterior of your office, what impression do they get? What does your office communicate to someone upon walking through the door? If you are home-based, take a walk in the shoes of a prospect or client as you enter your home-based operation. Are you maintaining a professional environment? What impression do the people associated with your business make? Your employees? Your vendors? You? Do you have an expectation of how someone associated with your business is to dress and present themselves on your behalf?

Visual Image: This is the graphic image of your company including your logo, brochures, website, and any other materials that promote your business visually. Make a list of words that describe how you want your ideal target market to think of your business when they see your logo or materials. Does it accomplish a majority of these impressions? Based on the words on your list, do the typestyles support the image you are trying to create? Are you using the same typestyles and logo consistently on all your promotional materials? What are your company colors and what impression do they make? Are the photo images and graphics used on your materials distinguishing you by helping tell a visual story about your business? Are they relevant and distinctive for your business?

Verbal Image: This is what you say about your business as well as what is written in your promotional materials. Do you have a strong mission and position for your business that sets you apart from your competition? Do you clearly state your offerings in terms of benefits specific to the markets you serve? Do you have a 30-second elevator talk that gets people's attention because it is about the difference you make for your customers rather than just listing your capabilities?

Personal Image: This is all about the experience you create for customers when they do business with you. What do you want your customer to personally take away and share with others? What experience do you create starting with the initial contact? What are your values and philosophy about doing business and how does this appeal and speak to your customers on a personal level? How does the experience and environment you create in your business affect employees? This last aspect is the critical differentiator for growth companies. So critical in fact, that it is further expanded upon in Secret #2.

In the CRISP Principle study, approximately 60 percent of companies that suffered negative or stagnant growth said they had a logo graphic and positioning for their company. However, in looking at how these companies answered other questions, they were not consistent in taking their image to the physical and personal level. In most cases, the personal experience aspect was not considered at all.

Minding your image is among the most important factors in building a business that stands the test of time. Longevity in business can always be tracked back to an understanding the importance of building and living up to one's image, reputation, and promises. By bringing all aspects of your image into sync, it will become a brand to be reckoned with in the marketplace.

> *While 60% of stagnant or negative growth companies claimed to have a logo graphic and positioning for their business, they typically were not using them consistently or correctly. Most also had no idea of the personal experience aspect of their business — or even what it was.*

Feeling the Heat

A propane gas company owned by a husband and wife team was six months into its operation and feeling the heat from competitors that had been in business for 30 years. They were in a price-driven commodity business. To make the challenge even more daunting, they had a two-year non-compete agreement that eliminated the ability to go after a large share of customers in their immediate service area. Their strategy had to focus on building awareness to attract customers to their company. During a strategy session to help build a plan to overcome these obstacles, their brand and how it was going to evolve was discussed. Being a home-based operation, they understood the importance of their visual and physical image. They had done an excellent job developing a distinctive logo with corporate colors and were consistently using them on their delivery vehicle, uniforms, and promotional materials. Missing from these efforts was a strong verbal message coupled with the experience their customers could expect by doing business with them. They embraced the process and launched out with the positioning, "Propane is propane. Service is everything!" They implemented grassroots core marketing initiatives to get their brand into the marketplace with exceptional results. Just 18 months after launching their campaign, readers of a weekly newspaper voted them the best propane gas company in the area. Their efforts paid off with growth that has allowed them to operate with multiple vehicles serving an expanded area.

•　　　•　　　•

Ask yourself what you want to communicate with your physical, visual, verbal and personal image. Unsure of some of the answers? Ask your best resources — your employees, community, suppliers and, most important of all, prospects and customers.

2

Memorable Experience

As mentioned in Secret #1, the critical differentiator between no-growth companies and high-growth companies is the ability to incorporate the experiential aspect into their branding strategy. They understood that creating a memorable and appealing experience for all who interact with the business sets it apart from all others. To get started, you should be able to confidently state your philosophy, values, approach, emotional appeal and desired outcomes.

Philosophy: What is your philosophy regarding how others should be treated? How is this incorporated into how you interact and do business with your customers, vendors and employees?

Values: What are your values? Your customers' values? How do your personal values affect the way you do business? Do you respect these values when you work with customers and others?

Approach: How is what you do different from your competitors? How do you approach working with customers and doing business? How will customers' experiences be different – and preferable – from what they experience with your competitors?

Emotional Appeal: How does it feel to do business with you? What emotions do you hope to inspire when others do business with you? How do you hope your products, services or capabilities make others feel when using them?

Outcomes: What are you ultimately trying to achieve for your customer? How are you trying to benefit them? What do customers say about doing business with you? Is it an inspired answer or simply a process-and-approach answer?

High Expectations

When a country club chef opened his own restaurant in 2001, he knew he wanted a destination restaurant, one where ambiance and experience combined with unique, artfully presented contemporary French cuisine for a memorable evening. It started off on rocky ground as 9-11 shook the nation during its first week in business, but the chef and his small support staff were determined to rise above the aftermath. And they did. By serving hot food on hot plates and cold food on cold plates and focusing on hundreds of other little details, the culinary team demonstrated they knew a customer's experience needed to be masterfully executed with a high level of comfort – not with snobbery. Surprise samples were delivered by servers from the Chef for a patron to share feedback or to cleanse the palate for the next course. Servers not only knew the menu and extensive wine list inside and out, but were also knowledgeable about happenings around the city to guide guests to the best after-dinner night spots. Being located in a corporate office building, A consultant helped the owner see the value in this situation. Breakfast and lunch became prime opportunities to set the stage for what people could expect if returning for dinner. Tracking results helped them know this worked as 65 percent of their business was repeat business. Corporate catering also accounted for 25 percent of its business as a result of their reputation for fine cuisine, wines and knowing how to wow guests. In the recent economic upheaval that left high-end restaurants across the country with significantly reduced revenues, this establishment experienced its best month in November 2009 and a 20 percent increase in the first quarter of 2010. This occurred in spite of several competing restaurants with more than 2,000 seats opening within walking distance. This award-winning restaurant and wine bar is the only establishment in its "Queen" city to receive the Wine Spectator's Award of

> **Whether you are a shareholder of one in your business or trying to keep multiple shareholders happy, never underestimate the power and impact the experience you create and manage has on differentiating your business and keeping customers and employees engaged.**

Excellence, proving that fine dining without the attitude
is the ultimate way to be successful.

•   •   •

Every business should define what it wants everyone who interacts with the business to experience. This is true for a business-to-business operation as well as a business-to-consumer enterprise. Taking stock of how your business creates and maintains a distinctive customer experience will strengthen not only your brand and image, but also your bottom line.

3
Beyond Capabilities

Many who launched their own businesses after working in Corporate America did so because they felt there had to be a better way. Those of you competing against Corporate America believe the same thing: you can do it better. One area where Corporate America has gotten it wrong is in the company mission statement. So wrong in fact, that whenever I propose developing a mission statement to clients or mention it in a marketing class I'm teaching, anyone who has worked for big business rolls their eyes in a "here we go again" mannerism.

So, if it's being done all wrong, is it really that important? The answer is "Yes." It is important once you start viewing it in the right way. Where Corporate America has gone astray is that most mission statements read like glorified capabilities statements. Check out enough websites where mission statements are posted and you will see what I mean. Many of them start with "To provide …" or "To be …" then only add a list of capabilities with claims of best quality and exceptional customer service thrown in for good measure.

This says nothing and means nothing. Most importantly, it inspires nothing. The key is to start thinking in terms of why you serve your ideal target market and what they will ultimately realize as a result. It's not what you do, but why you do it. Why are you serving your customer base? What are you trying to do for them that they cannot realize anywhere else?

A true mission statement will empower you to grow your business. If you have merely a capabilities statement as your mission statement, then you are only focusing on what you currently offer. A mission statement driven by purpose places you in a continuous growth mode rather then merely "doing what you do." It inspires new capabilities, products and innovations as you live your mission on a daily basis. Your mind will literally be opened to opportunities for achieving your mission beyond what you currently do. As a result, you'll continually expand your business.

High-growth companies understand the power of having a strong mission statement and take it very seriously. To help you understand the difference between a mission done wrong and a mission done right, let me share some examples of big businesses that have gotten it right. Coincidentally, these companies started out as entrepreneurial enterprises, which is not surprising.

Ben & Jerry's is a business that gets it and has not fallen into the corporate mindset trap. Their ultimate purpose and focus is about improving the quality of life for children and families, the environment, and sustainable family farms. But wait a minute you say, they make ice cream. Ice cream is what they do, not why they are doing what they do. They have understood from the very beginning that they are driven by more than ice cream. They've even gone so far as to create missions within their mission to address the different populations they serve. None of these are about what they do, but why they do it on a daily basis. This is what missions are made of in their finest sense.

Google is another company that gets it. Providing universal access to the world's information at a click is based on the user's ultimate convenience, with the consumer's impatience being at the core of why they do what they do. Notice how proudly Google displays that the search took a nanosecond to find thousands of possibilities? Their mission continuously pushes them to offer advancements and enhancements that provide instant gratification and results without delay.

In both these examples, the businesses began to formulate its mission by first understanding and defining its true purpose for existing. If you don't have a mission statement for your business, then it could be part of the reason you are floundering when it comes to making strategic decisions. If you do have a mission statement, then assess it to make sure you are not just regurgitating what you do with a few fluffy words.

> *A true mission statement conveys a meaningful, relevant reason that your business exists. When it does, it will continuously present a world of opportunities for your business to expand. Best of all, it will give your business a distinctive competitive advantage.*

Power of Purpose: What is your ultimate purpose for being in business? It's an easy question to answer if you begin by considering why you started your business in the first place. Chances are you had an impassioned idea that propelled you into business ownership because you knew you could make a difference. Now you just need to get to the core and essence of what this is for you and your business. What is your business ultimately doing for your customer as a result of the products and services you offer? What are you helping your customers realize, experience or achieve?

People-Centric Focus: Are you keeping your customer at the center of why you do what you do? Are you taking into consideration how your mission also affects and inspires your employees and anyone associated with your business? Your mission should inspire excitement in your employees and customers. They will become impassioned right along with you and share it with others because they can relate.

Distinctive Positioning: Does your mission support how you are different in what you do and why you do it? Does it help set you apart from your competition? Having a true mission that addresses a void, need or desire will distinguish you and make your business one that customers want to know more about. The best part of having a powerful purpose as the foundation of your mission is that it also will inspire how you position your company and its products and services against competitors. You can then take it one step further through a tagline or slogan that creatively brings your mission to life in a distinctive and memorable way.

Inspires Products or Services: The most powerful aspect of having a true mission is that it puts you in a more strategic mindset. As a result, you will be able to identify products or services you can add before your competitors do in an effort to fulfill your mission and better serve your customer.

Turning DIY into Profits

A graphic designer/copywriter realized shortly after going into business that her small business owner clients were not just in need of graphics expertise to create brochures and promotional materials. They were also starved for knowledge on how to best market their businesses in general. Seeing the opportunity to be a resource, she went back to school to learn more about marketing and public relations. Interestingly, her clients would ask her to share her lessons with them as she continued her studies. As a result, a mission was born: "To help business owners become savvier marketers in their business." In the late 1980s, the personal computer and desktop publishing craze hit the business world. Many business owners began creating their own brochures and newsletters in-house to save money. Because of her mission, the graphic designer immediately invested in a PC to supplement her Mac computer. She then expanded her service offerings to include coaching and consulting to serve as a creative director and copy editor to business owners wishing to do the bulk of their promotional materials themselves. Many graphic designers lost clients as a result of this "do it yourself" evolution within the small business sector. By 1990 her graphic

design business had grown and expanded into a full-
service marketing, consulting, coaching and services
support firm demonstrating how a powerful mission can
provide a competitive advantage.

●　　　●　　　●

The best part about knowing this secret is that many of your competitors have also remained caught in the old mindset. So while they are still just focusing on their capabilities and what they do, you can attract customers because of why you exist especially for them!

4

Budgeting for Growth

In times of economic unrest, tightening purse strings is a common source of tension. For small business owners, watching every penny is an everyday challenge. Amazingly, while many small business owners carefully consider all their expenses, many do not operate from a formal budget. Additionally, those who do have a budget are short-sighted, only looking at what business is costing them now, rather than anticipating costs based on their growth plans.

High-growth companies anticipate budget needs, consider all the resources in their budget, and implement initiatives in phases based a long-term budget projections according to planned growth. Here's a look at what this means.

Anticipating Needs: Does this sound like you? You have defined sales and expansion goals, but do you have goals regarding the capacity, equipment, people, and support you also need to fulfill the orders? High-growth companies anticipate what will be needed to accommodate their growth. By doing this, it actually forces a company to validate its projected numbers. When you say you want to increase sales by a certain percentage, how will it affect your need for staffing and support once you have the business in hand? You'll set better sales goals if you understand the expected operational investments that will also be required.

All Resources Considered: If you believe money is the only resource you have to budget, then you have closed many doors to growing your business the smart way. You actually have four resources that need to be used and budgeted wisely in your business. These resources are time, people, technology, and money. They all need to be considered and allocated on a regular basis, not just during an economic wake-up call.

- <u>Time:</u> Time is consistently an undervalued asset even though everyone wishes they had more of it. Growth companies consider time and how it is spent by everyone associated with the company as a precious asset.

- <u>People:</u> People are not just your employees. They can also mean other companies and *their* people working for you. Outsourcing to others is also an option. This can help you focus on more income-generating activities while other people are handling the necessary support aspects of your business.

- Technology: Technology saves you people, time and money. Looking for ways to use technology for greater efficiency is time well spent and will save you time and money later on.

- Money: Then, of course, there is money. Growth companies understand that by leveraging the first three resources more effectively, they are making wiser decisions about where to spend money.

Phased Implementation: Many business owners are afraid to know how much it will cost to promote and market their business. So, they tend not to budget at all, thinking they'll spend money when they can afford to spend it. The problem with this approach is that it is not based on strategy or truly knowing what it is going to take to effectively market the company. You need to make sure you are marketing on an ongoing basis with whatever capacity you have. The best thing you can do is develop a strategy and then prepare a plan that includes ALL the costs associated with the time, technology, people and money needed to implement. Your budget gives you a basis for knowing at what capacity you can begin. Phasing enables you to proactively keep your marketing efforts going.

> *Waiting until you can afford to market is like waiting until you can afford to have a baby. Giving birth to this baby called your business will not help it grow or develop any more than giving birth to a child helps her or him grow. It takes resources and a concerted effort.*

Growth companies are able to strategically prioritize initiatives and plan a phased implementation. You can do this too. By having a clear picture of what every tactic and initiative will cost in time, people, technology and money, you can determine implementation phases based on short-term and long-term goals and your immediate objectives. Typically, a short-term goal is one that can be achieved more quickly for a faster return on investment. For instance, if one of your short term goals is to increase repeat business of your existing customer base, then the tactics associated with it should be placed within your first phase of implementation.

Targeted Implementation: Even when using your resources more effectively, you will not be able to implement all of your initiatives if you have a wide market area. So, you must target your resources for the greatest return on investment. Whether your geographic focus is national, regional, or local, there are ways you can be more targeted in where you budget your resources for a higher impact result. Secret #5 on profit sizing, Secret #8 on trends, and Secret #19 on segmenting and targeting tell you how you can be more focused in your implementation. The key is and always will be the strategy behind what you are doing. Concentrating efforts within pockets of geographic or target market sectors will reap a more significant return compared to a more blanketed approach.

Clean Sweep

By spending lots of time but little money, a junk-removal services company used grassroots marketing to create awareness and interest when it first opened its doors. Everything from door hangers and trucks serving as hard-to-miss traveling billboards to strategically placed yard and intersection signage, pounding the pavement in a variety of ways put the company's name continually in front of people. Three years later, when the company began offering franchises, marketing required a more sophisticated operational approach with a wider reach to support multiple locations and larger metropolitan areas. However, as the economy slowed, the approach was proving costly and didn't achieve the desired results. Rolling up their sleeves, the leadership team analyzed what had worked and what hadn't. They realized that the key to owning a market was to focus on highly targeted pockets within a metropolitan area, not attempting to reach the entire area. With a priority list of 10 tactics that had proven effective across numerous markets, the company rolled out a plan for franchisees with phenomenal success. First, they sought out areas with a high mix of residential and commercial development within one square mile. Then, the franchisees were instructed to conduct a wave of promotions within this concentrated area for high exposure and impact over three-week periods. To promote a junk pick-up day to area residents and business owners, fliers were distributed by posting them at coffee shops and grocery stores in the area. Franchise employees would stand at strategic intersections waving signs that focused on educating people about how the company could help a family or business. Signs read "Car won't fit in garage?" or "Need yard cleaned up?" The idea was to solidify each franchise's position as the neighborhood junk removal and services company while making marketing dollars go further. A venture that started out as a group of college guys earning summer-break money by hauling junk evolved into an Inc. 500 company by staying true to what made the junk removal franchise operation a success from the beginning.

High-growth business owners put their plans into action rather than waiting until they can afford it because they determine a budget, consider all available resources, and then implement it in phases with targeted finesse.

•   •   •

After you have developed a strategy and action plan for your company, sit down with your team and develop a resources budget. Work with your accountant to develop a financial budget on how you will use all your resources more effectively. Then implement your plan based on a budget that works for you in the short and long-term.

5
Profit Sizing

Do you feel you are working harder for less profit? Are you frustrated by the current economy and the competitive environment that are unlike any previous time in history? Are you feeling pressure to adjust your pricing under the guise of getting more customers? Before you let these conditions steer your decision-making, take time to "profit size" your business.

What is profit sizing? It is a strategic analysis of your target market segments, your products and services, and your geographic concentration areas to ensure that you are focusing your marketing efforts where the most profits and sales will be created. It will also help you identify areas that are not profitable or are eating away at your profits. Once this is done, you will be better able to prioritize where your marketing efforts should focus, and eliminate segments, capabilities or geographic regions that no longer contribute to your bottom line.

Target Industry/Niche Analysis: Make a list of your customer segments either by niche or by industry, whichever is best suited to your business. If you are not clear on what this means, Secret #19 goes into more detail. After you have made this list, use the following criteria to identify the segments that present the greatest opportunity for increasing sales and profits:

- Most profitable to do business with
- Your company's proven track record to serve
- Least labor intensive to serve
- Likelihood to utilize multiple products/services
- Most likely to value service & support
- Most likely to give referrals
- Highest level of expertise & competency
- Potential to continually add products/services
- Opportunities to expand beyond current customer base

Take a look at your responses and see which segments match the majority of these areas and which ones fall short.

Automagic Pricing & Profits

A remanufactured ink cartridge business owner had experienced steady growth since starting the business in 1991 because of her focus on green/sustainability and quality. Her business grew on a double-digit level through 2007 when a shift began. Pricing wars became the norm as more competitors entered into the remanufactured ink cartridge business. The business was not as profitable as the owner knew it could be. In addition, when bid opportunities came in, it took days to determine the final pricing, which cost money in many ways. She did some due diligence and calculated that poor data management cost her company $278,000 in profit over a 12-month period. Refusing to do battle based on price alone with competitors, the owner decided to focus on putting systems into place that maintained quality standards, elevated customer service initiatives and better monitored profitability and manufacturing costs to determine competitive, yet profitable pricing. She wanted a pricing and profitability platform that would consider market-down and cost-up comparisons in pricing. The entire industry, including her own estimators, was basing pricing on cost-up versus market-down. This needed to change. In addition, conversion manufacturing times and parts costs were not efficiently being calculated into the end pricing and profit numbers. Competitor pricing combined with quality comparisons were also not being analyzed thoroughly. She was told there was no existing program that could incorporate this amount of data. She believed otherwise. She could see it in her head and knew it could

High-growth companies continue to grow in spite of an economic downturn because they understand how to profit size their business according to market conditions and opportunities that exist on a targeted strategic level. The real secret is to do this continually even when times are good.

be done. Once she defined all the data feeds she
ultimately wanted the system to manage, she hired an
employee totally dedicated to custom building this
program. Over the course of 18 months, the data was
researched, verified and incorporated into a single
spreadsheet. The Quoter, as they dubbed the system,
enables the company to generate a spreadsheet for
competitive price and profitability comparisons. Once
these are generated, a customer-ready PDF document is
"automagically" produced for submittal. In addition, an
automated customer order and usage tracking system was
implemented that enables her team to know exactly when
a new order needs to be placed. A call is made and buyers
are amazed by how accurate the remanufacturer's
customer service employees are able to anticipate a new
order. Customers never run out of ink cartridges because
this supplier has their back. As a result of these and
other new systems, the company is on track for growth
that will reach triple digits with national contracts. And
it all came about by understanding where and how
profits are made.

Product / Services Analysis: Make a list of all your products and services and rate each one based on profitability, distinctiveness, least labor intensive, etc. to identify which ones should get the top priority in your marketing efforts.

Should have low priority focus: Should have high priority focus:

- Least profitable
- Commodity/market saturated
- More labor intensive to deliver
- Decreasing demand/declining sales
- Price driven

- Most profitable
- Distinctive/fewer competitors
- Least labor intensive to deliver
- Increasing demand/growing sales
- Value driven

Did you discover you are investing marketing dollars, time, and energy into offerings that are not serving your bottom line? Are you hanging on to a product or service that may have served you well at one time, but is no longer the money maker it once was? Are some products and services taking your focus away from more profitable offerings? Don't be fooled into believing that offering a low price enticement will ultimately result in profits. Small business simply cannot compete on a pricing platform, especially in a down economy.

Geographic Segmentation Analysis: Too often marketing dollars are spent attempting to cover an overall geographic area, be it local, regional, national or international. A more strategic approach is to identify those pockets of opportunity within your geographic footprint that will give you the greatest concentration of increased customers who want your most profitable offerings.

Take a look at your overall geographic service area. Then assess and prioritize where to conduct marketing activity based on the following criteria:

- Concentration of most profitable target customer segments
- Least or fewer direct competitors in area
- Greatest ability to leverage existing relationships
- Greatest potential for strategic alliances for entry into area

When companies conduct a profit sizing analysis, they are better able to target their marketing efforts for a high concentration of frequency and impact that is more easily controlled and measured for results. Just like you personally can't be all things to all people, your business cannot be in all places at one time and make a lasting impression. Profit sizing enables you to focus on where you are most likely to sell your products and services for the greatest profit.

•   •   •

Profit sizing your business will help you make better decisions that increase profits along with sales. Chances are you will eliminate some customer segments, offerings, and geographic areas that were draining your profits. This will allow you to make even greater strides in those areas with the greatest potential for return on investment. So make profit sizing your business a part of your annual review of your marketing and operational strategy.

6
Sales is Not Marketing

Are you telling yourself that if everyone just pounds more pavement, you'll increase sales? If so, you are suffering from a sales mindset disguised as marketing. A sales force without marketing behind it is not a force. It is a farce. Marketing supports and enables sales to occur. Marketing energizes and inspires sales. Marketing attracts sales. Marketing is the foundation from which sales can blast off when done properly and in an ongoing strategic way.

High-growth companies get this in a big way. They understand that sales efforts are a part of marketing, and not the same thing as marketing. Consider these traps in thinking that could have you stuck in a sales mode versus a marketing mode.

Sales Calls versus Marketing: Numerous stagnant, negative-growth companies relied almost entirely on direct sales efforts, cold calling and telemarketing as the primary means of gaining business. While the hard-sell, transaction mentality may have worked in the past, high-growth companies understand that sales happen as a result of solving problems, anticipating needs and wowing customers. They are not just selling a product or service; they are fulfilling a void in the marketplace. Effectively communicating this through marketing initiatives and materials that support the sales force is critical to converting prospects into customers.

Sales Leads versus Qualified Buyers: I have a problem with the term sales leads. Why? Because as far as I am concerned, a sales lead is a rumor. It is certainly better than a cold call because at least there is some data indicating they are among your ideal market. But the reality is, without knowing more, this prospect is no more than a possibility, and a questionable one at that. When a sales effort is supported by an ongoing targeted strategy, qualified buyers inquire. They are attracted to do business with your company. Sales leads need to be pursued. Which would you prefer? A sales effort that can immediately focus on closing the sale because customers are attracted to the business or a sales team out chasing the sale?

Sales Team versus Strategic Team: High-growth companies understand that sales are only one spoke in the marketing strategy wheel. The sales force is a valued part of the marketing initiative and provides valuable input into the marketing efforts. They are taught to be strategists first in how they think and approach making a sale. A strategy-minded sales force is focused on establishing and developing relationships and serving the customer as a whole. They understand what these relationships mean for the company's long-term success.

Mind Shift

When co-founders of a national real estate firm initially started their company, they envisioned a different type of real estate franchise operation. The founders had owned highly successful and profitable real estate franchises themselves and wanted to put their methodologies into practice in this new venture. They would provide a better way to approach selling real estate. The key to their strategy was in developing agents and brokers who would embrace the markets they served rather than just working the markets where they lived, relying on a company brand to bring in business. The leadership knew from experience that real estate buyers and sellers do not choose a real estate agent based on the real estate company name. With commissions turning real estate sales into a commodity business, the reason an agent is preferred over another is based on the agent's local reputation, knowledge of the local real estate marketplace, their sphere of influence and ability to deliver. Therefore, instead of investing financial resources in national branding advertising campaigns, this company focused on investing in training and coaching its agent partners to become the best real estate business people they could be, not just sales people. This meant helping agents become market strategists, real estate analysts, marketing mavericks and exceptional

> *If your sales people are telling you that you need to do more marketing so they can sell more effectively and you are telling them to bring in more sales for you to afford to do more marketing, then it's time for a reality check. You have been confusing your sales activity with marketing effectively.*

service agents who delivered as promised. The leadership knew that this approach would differentiate the company against stiff competition within each local market level. While competing agents were caught in the sales mentality of waiting for the phone to ring, their agents would be positioning themselves as the best choice through analyzing and assessing local market conditions, targeting and segmenting leads and prospects, anticipating market shifts and trends and building relationships. As the economy continued to move towards recession status, the leadership knew that a paradigm shift needed to happen and they were the ones who could do it. Having experienced a few downturns since the company was established in 1983, the founders and leadership team had already proven what worked and this meant adapting ahead of the market in order to rule each marketplace. A marketing training initiative was put into practice across the country specifically focused on tackling tough economic times. Incorporated into training programs throughout the franchise, and then captured in a book released in 2009, agents learned 12 critical tactics that showed them how to shift their thinking and the way they had been approaching real estate during booming times. While the real estate industry shrunk as a whole by 10 percent, this education-focused and strategy-minded company enjoyed its most profitable year to date in 2009. Agents had embraced the power that comes from knowing when you put a business and strategic mindset behind sales, you get results. Best of all, their satisfied clients and communities are also smiling as these agents helped them do what others said couldn't be done because they were telling everyone that "we just need to wait out the downturn."

Sales Tunnel versus Marketing Funnel: When you have a strategic marketing program in place, it will funnel opportunities to your sales team. The high-growth company focuses on supporting sales efforts with a strong, cohesive marketing strategy, which in turn makes sales easier. If your marketing efforts rely solely on sales people or on you personally "making the sale," then you are caught in a trap where you are working harder to get through to a prospective customer, not smarter. Marketing enables you to shift your efforts from convincing a prospect to do business with you to getting down to the specific ways you will serve the prospect. You no longer need to convince them. You are inspiring them to do business with you. You respond to their specific interests based on how the marketing funnel attracted them in the first place.

•   •   •

Shifting from a sales-only mentality to a true marketing strategy will prove more valuable than you can possibly imagine until you do it. What makes it even better is that your sales force will run circles around your competition because you have made it so easy to sell what you offer. Start seeing your sales team's efforts as a component of marketing. Seek their input so you can develop a marketing program that drives sales opportunities to you instead of you having to pursue them.

7

Strategy into the Plan

Having a plan does not guarantee success. More than 60 percent of negative or stagnant-growth companies in our study claimed they had a marketing plan. Clearly, just having a plan was not the key to success. Using a well-formulated strategy to create the plan and then implementing the plan is the key.

What would happen if you bought a piece of equipment, but didn't plug it in? Absolutely nothing. It would sit idle. What would happen if you hired a person for a job and didn't tell them where they were going to work? They wouldn't show up. What would happen if you scheduled a trip, but had no way of getting there? You'd never reach your destination.

Of course, you wouldn't buy a machine without plugging it in, hire a person without telling them where they will work, or schedule a trip without a way to get there. Yet, time after time, business owners develop a marketing and business plan without a strategy. Furthermore, it isn't plugged into the company's day-to-day operations, isn't put to work in the marketplace, and doesn't use vehicles to get customers to their desired destinations.

There is a clear difference between companies that grew despite economic downturns and those that didn't. It is how they prepared their business and marketing plans. Here are some of the reasons why plans of stagnant, negative-growth companies fell short.

Field of Dreams Mentality: In our study, 66 percent of stagnant, negative-growth companies claimed they had developed a brand and positioning for their company as part of their marketing plan. So why didn't sales happen? Upon further investigation, we found two very striking reasons. The first was what I equate to getting all dressed up to go out, and then staying home to eat a TV dinner. Some of these companies may have invested a lot of time and money in their image, but they were not putting it out there for people to get to know and experience. They literally had a Field of Dreams mentality of "if we build it, they will come." The second discovery was based on other answers to other questions in the survey. These companies did not have an image or positioning that distinguished them or spoke to their market. Don't just create an image for your company, create one that says you are different and the best choice. Then develop a strategy to get the image out into the marketplace so your company will become known and respected. And also one your target market will be proud to experience.

React & Protect Mentality: If you are continuously responding and trying to keep up, then you are likely operating without a plan or a strategy. The main benefit of operating with a strategy in place is that you can be proactive instead of reactive. You can actively anticipate possible scenarios. Especially during slow economic times, savvy companies have two strategies in place based on which way the market shifts. A solid strategy requires you to look at some critical situations within your business. These include exploring trends, competitors, opportunities, challenges, pricing, and the current state of your business operations. Do you have a strategy that addresses all of these areas in detail? Do you honestly know where your business currently is so you can effectively plan where it needs to go?

Steady Grows

When a training and process documentation business owner established her company in 1990, she knew it would be a dynamic business, continually evolving in step with what her target markets would accept and continue to buy. From the onset, a strategy was in place to keep a pulse on her business segments to make decisions based on where learning and business processes were moving. By 1997, her business had grown to 20 people with a solid base as a preferred supplier to Fortune 500 clients in the Southeast. She also realized the company had outgrown its name, so she developed a strategy based on a new brand image and expanded focus as a manager of critical business information. Although continuing to see steady double-digit growth, she realized that for her company to become a global provider, it needed to evolve beyond the confines of her own knowledge base. Her company needed to shift from being an owner-driven business to one with a sales engine and expertise driven by a leadership team, not

> **More than 60 percent of stagnant, negative-growth companies in the study said they had a marketing plan and yet did not grow. The reason many plans are created and not implemented is because they just include a list of numerous tasks on paper. Without a strategy behind a plan, there is no driving force behind it.**

just by her. This team would be critical to taking the company to its next level, one that required not just practitioners, but stakeholders and crafters of the company's strategy with a collaborative interest in its success. A dream team was assembled in 2007 and the company's base of knowledge and capability evolved once again into a provider of learning and content management strategists, consultants and project managers. The owner was no longer the core expert, but one of many bringing high level competency to clients throughout the eastern U.S. Her strategy paid off when a key client merged with a competitor. While the merger resulted in many suppliers being eliminated or replaced, her company saw expanded demand from the new entity. A second location was established to better serve the needs of this key client while also putting the company in a strategic location for gaining more clients west of the Mississippi. With 49 people and a solid leadership team, this 20 year-old company proves that steady growth requires a revised strategy at every step and a visionary who can get out of the way to allow others to help the company evolve.

Ready, Fire, Aim Mentality: Why will a business owner spend hours laboring over the right phone system, yet will impulsively purchase an ad like a bar of candy at a checkout line? The no-growth companies in our study tended to put all their eggs in one basket and then coupled this with a sporadic, impulsive approach to what they did. Growth companies have a strategy that demonstrates a mix of tactics in their marketing efforts on an ongoing basis rather than a sporadic basis or single-tactic focus. They incorporate multiple levels of core initiatives and then augment them with highly targeted supplemental initiatives, when necessary. The next six sections in this book offer multiple aspects of core and supplemental initiatives for you to implement in your business. In the "CRISP Principle: The Study" section of the book, you were introduced to the five core initiatives every business needs to use.

The investments business owners make are critical to the ultimate success and growth of their business. Investing time and energy around a strategy is critical to revving up the engine behind your business and marketing plan. Without strategy, there is no plan. Once you start thinking strategically, you will be amazed how far it will take you. You will make better marketing and operational investment decisions and will also know with confidence what is right and not right for your business.

What goes into your strategy is even more important than having a strategy mindset to begin with. Now that we have identified the common pitfalls when companies don't have a strategy, let's take a look at what you need to consider in your strategy.

Best Value Offense: If you have taken the time to define your mission and ultimate purpose, you should be able to pinpoint what your best value offense will be in your business. There are three offenses you can take in your business: Best Product or Service. Best Total Solutions, and Best Price. Strategically, you want to excel against your competitors in one of them. You should strive to be at par with competitors and slightly better, if possible, at a second one. The remaining offense you don't make a priority or a focus. It is impossible to do all three well, hence why you focus on a priority of two. You need to begin with identifying what your competitors are doing and how they are prioritizing these three areas. To your delight, you may find some competitors not doing a very good job of this. To help you assess competitors as well as your own business, here is a brief description of each value offense.

- Best Product or Service: Having the best product or service is exactly what it says. You are providing the very best. From a product standpoint, it can mean high performance or the highest quality compared to any other product on the market. From a service standpoint, it means you will provide service better than any other company. Best service as a focus could also be the most innovative or creative. How you define this level of service is based on what is most important to your customer as well as what you are willing to do. You may offer a guarantee, warranty or money back if a customer is not satisfied. Companies with the best quality product or service as their primary focus also win awards and gain continuous testimony from customers and the marketplace.

- Best Total Solutions: When you are focused on total solutions, you are dedicated to being a total resource and solutions provider to your customer. This does not mean you offer every solution under the sun, but that you are committed to offering solutions that go above and beyond competitors' offerings. You desire to be the go-to company, making it your business to know your customers intimately. You anticipate their needs and direct them to other resources as a value-added aspect of doing business with you. You may even go as far as to qualify other service or product providers as a means of assuring any resource will be a good fit for the customer.

- Best Price: Best price is the most difficult area for small business to effectively compete. Best price is about being the least expensive. It often includes offering your product or service fast and cheap. It can also be cheap as a result of being ganged in production with other product orders, so the customer must wait longer than normal to receive the special pricing. Just because your competitors, especially larger ones, are competing on price, it does not mean you must slash your prices. In *every* product or service category, there is a market where price is not the main deciding factor. Identify these more ideal customers and then focus on how you can be a solutions provider and/or quality provider.

Entre Donners

A firm of impassioned engineers were determined when establishing their consulting firm not to just be entrepreneurs for its stable of clients, but to be "entre donners." In French "preneur" means taker while "donner" means to give. For these business-minded problem-solvers, this meant giving value. So they embarked on making this a standard within their company from the very beginning. In the small niche markets it serves, the firm's goal is to position itself as the place to go for solutions and earn respect in each marketplace. Its vision is to be known for its ability to solve problems with their thin film solutions by digging deeper into what a client is truly trying to achieve with their end products. By being one with a client's mission, they deliver more than just a solution. They bring value that will translate into an ongoing partnership with the client as new challenges are identified. For the high performance auto racing client, this means durable parts to finish the race and more horse power to the rear wheels to ultimately win the race. Through this firm's ingenuity, films used two years ago have become obsolete as better films continue to be developed as demand increases based on the customer's growing need for more horsepower. This means this firm must work in advance to stay ahead of the racer's next requirement. Because the engineering team does this so well, customers know this company will be ready for their "What's next" because they are being viewed as a strategic partner in helping them stay ahead of the pack. Also progressive thinkers, the team of engineers are driven by finding solutions to problems that have not occurred yet. This has been especially valued in the medical niches they serve. Their methodology combined with forward thinking has brought theory and practice together with astounding results. Through testing the science, then the medical efficacy, then its ability to go to market in partnership with clients, a coherent idea manifests into an out-of-the-box design becoming a reality in their life-giving and life-saving products. From orthopedic to organ transport solutions, this firm continues to push the envelope in building technical solutions that no one else is creating. Their tenacity in finding solutions may mean changing course many times, but for the medical client it was always ultimately about what the end result would mean to the patient, their families and the medical community. As the economy shifted, while competitors began to conduct fear-based price cutting, they tightened their scope of focus to markets where their value-based pricing would win the project. Dropping off less profitable clients and exchanging other clients to better competitive fits, they increased their pricing and margins. With 30 percent growth from 2007 through 2010 and a 19 percent growth rate going into its next fiscal year, this engineering firm proves that their approach of giving value above and beyond what can be imagined is the "entredonnerial" thing to do.

Situation Analysis: This is a critical part of your strategy that looks at the current state of your business and your industry are currently. Included in your situation analysis should be an overview of your company and its history, a review of your direct and indirect competitors, their strengths, weaknesses and positioning in the marketplace. Pricing and profitability strategies should be explored compared to competitors.

Vision, Mission, & Offerings: Without defining a mission and vision for your company, it will be difficult for you to differentiate your company or evolve your offerings beyond what you currently offer. This was described in more detail in Secret #3.

Opportunities (Current and Future): The action plan within your strategy should focus on opportunities. These may be determined based on trends (Secret #8), new products or capabilities (Secrets #10 and #11), ways you choose to serve your ideal target market (Secrets #13 - #21), and areas your competitors may not be focusing on or doing effectively (Secrets #1 - #50).

Challenges & Considerations: Like it or not, running a business has its challenges. If your strategy is not addressing them, you are like an ostrich with your head in the sand. Solid strategies identify the challenges and obstacles that can have a negative impact on marketing or operations. Forward-thinking strategies also offer solutions or counterpoints to each challenge or obstacle. This means that you have not only acknowledged the challenges, but have assessed them and identified solutions, contingencies and ways to turn them into opportunities.

Goals Beyond Sales: In Secret #6, we discussed goals that center around increasing sales. An effective strategy also considers goals that focus on your operations. If you reach the level of sales you have targeted, will additional people, equipment or resources be needed? For example, when an engineering firm analyzed its sales goals, it discovered that if these sales goals were achieved, an additional project manager and lab technician would need to be hired and an investment would need to be made in lab equipment to ensure the capacity to complete the work at the higher sales level. This is why it is important to understand how sales are going to be achieved and what will need to happen operationally to support successful sales.

Action Plan for Implementation: The action plan is what will put the strategy into motion. It will include a timeline and who is responsible for execution in various phases. It will be organized according to priorities based on budgeted resources. It should be referenced often and used as a guide for tracking results.

•　　•　　•

If the idea of developing a strategy is overwhelming, seek assistance. It is that important. If you need some guidance before hiring an outside firm, seek out a Small Business Development Center or other small business resource programs associated with the U.S. Small Business Administration. These centers and programs often include free counseling and numerous resources to help you.

8
Trend Getters

Are you a step ahead or trying to keep up? Trends can help you differentiate and identify needs like nothing else can. Too many business owners don't look at trends or consider how they can be strategically leveraged. Even those who do consider trends will stop at the obvious and don't explore trends for the gold they can bring to their business.

Beyond Your Industry Trends: Too many businesses only look as far as their own industry to identify trends that they might be able to leverage in their business. Some of the most innovative ideas in business models, service offerings, or products were literally stolen and adapted from one industry to another. This is why subscribing to some form of communications that can feed you what is happening from a trend standpoint across all industries is a smart investment. Publications including the *Wall Street Journal*, *USA Today*, *Inc.* and *Entrepreneur* magazines are sharing trends to watch on a regular basis.

The Geography of Trends: If you have looked at trends within your industry and nothing more, then you may also be falling behind depending on where you are geographically located. I have a secret within this secret. Innovations within the U.S. tend to first occur in most industries on the West coast. They then travel to the Northeast and then settle into the Southeast. We only need to look at "going green" to see this is true. Californians were living green in the 1970's. It wasn't until the start of the 21st century that it hit the Southeast and the rest of the country in a big way. If you are in the Northeast, look to what companies like yours are doing in the West. If you are in the Southeast, look at what companies like yours are doing in the West or Northeast. If you are a global competitor or already located in the West, look at what businesses are doing in Europe in terms of product manufacturing or services and to Asia for what's going on in the technology or the alternative medicine front.

Consumer & Lifestyle Trends: Whether your company has a business-to-consumer focus or is a business-to-business company, the people you are seeking to purchase your products or services (even if they are a decision-maker within a company) are not only consumers, but individuals. Understanding consumer and lifestyle trends can help you better communicate and relate to the individuals within your ideal target market. Take a look at the common denominators of your decision-making market and if there are any trends occurring within that demographic segment. A good example is the Baby Boomer generation who are juggling parenting adult and younger children, being grandparents, and caring for their parents. A new multi-generational and inner-generational dynamic is affecting their lifestyle, including how they approach work. Businesses, products and services are being created at a monumental rate as this trend continues to play out.

Trend Benchmarking & Tracking: Using your own customer or client base as a study group can be a useful way to identify trends you can utilize to make better strategic decisions. Not only is this of value to your company, but also provides value-added proprietary insight to your customers that competitors can't provide. Conducting a survey among your customers to identify any trends or best practices can be an eye-opener.

If your target market is other businesses, conducting a survey with your customer's customer base can offer valuable insights that not only help you serve your customer's needs better, but also enable you to identify ways they can serve their customers better.

High-growth companies are often trend getters rather than trend setters. They understand how to identify and leverage trends in other industries or how to take advantage of shifting trends to suit their market's needs. While what is being introduced is not necessarily original, it is still new or of value to the market it serves.

From Patterns to Profits

From the inception of her company, a healthcare consultant and educator focused on niches as a means of effectively marketing and building a strong client base. Initially serving hospitals, she quickly evolved into working with physician practices in specialized areas. While there were other consultants focusing on niches within the industry, most of them operated in a reactionary mode. Organizations were either sold an overall packaged program or used the consultants as inspectors to identify problems from a regulatory or compliance standpoint. This consultant had a more visionary idea of what her company would bring to the marketplace. She would not just fix problems, but also anticipate and prevent issues through objective analysis of regulations. As someone who avidly studied the industry, she would conduct

*benchmarking and patterning analysis to identify trends
and opportunities. She first found success in identifying
trends occurring within a specific practice and then
advising them based on what she discovered. In
conducting benchmark studies among her various
clientele within their individual practices, she saw an
opportunity to take it to a more comprehensive level by
gaining permission to combine multiple practices into an
ongoing study to gain even more insight. The ability to
compare recurring issues and challenges among a
consortium of practices on an ongoing basis took her
ability to identify trends and patterns to a new level of
excellence. It also gave her an edge other consultants did
not have with hard data and insights not available
through any other source. Since establishing her
company in 1993, she has realized the power of not only
being a trend getter, but being a trend watcher, turning
patterns into profits for both her firm and her clients.
She is a nationally known expert and her firm continues
to enjoy double-digit growth amidst one of the most
challenging times in the healthcare industry.*

The reason I entitled this secret "Trend Getter" is because it's not just about blazing new paths or innovating something from nothing. Some high-growth companies are astute at envisioning new ways to approach and leverage what already exists.

Make trend watching a part of your business operations. Assign someone to gather information on trends and monitor them on an ongoing basis. Include trends in your strategic planning discussions. Don't let a shortage of time or people put this important secret on the back burner. College interns are a great use of the people source for trend watching and analysis.

•   •   •

Investigating and effectively leveraging trends is probably the most underutilized components of a marketing strategy. The greatest reason for being a trend watcher is that many of your competitors are not. There is no time like the present to make trend watching a powerful tactic to grow your business.

9

Investment vs. Expense

Is an expense mindset costing you? As a business owner, you've probably heard from customers making cutbacks: "I can't afford the expense at this time." The domino effect has likely caused you to begin to view everything as an expense as well. When times get tough, companies tend to curtail or cease spending altogether. Everything that costs money is viewed as an expense. If everything is viewed as an expense, then decisions are based not on a growth model but rather a survival model. Those who start a business wanting only to survive are sabotaging their ability to make sound, strategic decisions that will grow and sustain their businesses.

The key is to know and understand the difference between an expense and an investment in your business. In the research my firm released in 2004 comparing high-growth companies to stagnant, negative-growth companies during the 2002/2003 downturn after 9-11, growth companies continued to invest. High-growth companies understood the difference between an investment and an expense. It's important to note that this mindset was standard operating procedure for these companies. In spite of the economy, they simply continued doing what they knew was essential to their growth strategy.

They made strategic investments when times were good, remaining fiscally responsible by avoiding extravagances. This enabled them to continue making investments when the economic picture changed. The result cushioned the blow of the downturn and allowed them to grow. This is also holding true in the current economic malaise. These companies typically focused their investments in five areas: image and marketing, training and development, technology, physical location and hiring.

Image and marketing: If you feel you can't afford to market your business, then you can't afford to be in business. This is where stagnant and negative-companies go awry. When times were good, they stopped marketing despite the fact that it was marketing that made them busy in the first place. They became comfortable with business coming in, deeming that marketing was no longer necessary. Or they shifted to a servicing mode in order to meet their business commitments, so marketing took a back seat. A stop-and-go or stop-and-wait mentality regarding marketing will cause more business failures than anything else. Another reason marketing is viewed as an expense is because all too often, marketing dollars are not spent strategically or wisely. As a result, the money spent is viewed as a cost with no apparent return on investment. That only needs to happen a few times to make business owners foolishly think marketing dollars are an expense.

For growth companies, marketing is an ongoing investment and an operational part of how the company conducts business. These companies also understand that certain expenses are actually investments in disguise. When marketing efforts are strategic, companies make wiser decisions, thus assuring the money spent will get the desired return.

Driver's Seat

A pediatric equipment company had been allocating a flat-fee reimbursement for mileage and gas for the personally-owned vehicles of its direct sales force. While the reimbursement was considerate to the sales force, the personal vehicles were not able to effectively hold all the equipment or parts necessary for optimal in-service calls. In addition, the vehicles were unmarked and did not provide any marketing value while on the road. In late 2009, the company investigated leasing custom-adapted vans to replace personal vehicles. In January 2010, the first van was placed on the road in an expansion market. It was custom-fitted to better house the demonstration equipment and parts, and also reinforced the company brand and image. The results from the first van validated the shift to company-owned vehicles as a wise and strategic investment on several fronts.

> *Some business owners don't need an economic downturn to have an expense-only mind-set. Everything is viewed as an expense coming out of their own pocket to the point of crippling their ability to make good decisions. Are you a victim of this way of thinking?*

Training and development: Growth companies understand that to grow, attention must be paid to developing its employees. Investing in technical or soft skills training to enhance the capabilities of the organization's people makes a company a stronger competitor. From the ability to sell, negotiate, and more effectively use software or equipment to implementing a quality initiative, smart growth businesses understand they cannot grow if they do not make growing their people an ongoing investment. Especially in down times, programs to help people better cope with stress or to collaboratively work together with fewer people are deemed critical operational investments by companies that see their people as critical to the company's staying power and growth. This also gives the company an image boost with customers who view it as a good, stable place to do business with *and* a good place to work.

Lean & Green

A manufacturing company was enduring the cost of doing business resulting from pricing wars that impacted profitability. It became apparent that more efficiencies and less waste were paramount to operational sustainability. So the company invested in an overall plant-recycling and waste-reduction program that required training and the implementation of new processes. In addition, a lean manufacturing initiative was also put into place by key plant personnel, who received additional training to execute the program. The resulting efficiencies enabled the company to allocate money for an ongoing and more aggressive marketing program. Best of all, both initiatives offered the company important distinctions compared to its competitors in being lean, green and ready to produce and deliver.

Technology: When done strategically, technology is an investment that pays your business back in a multitude of ways. A business owner should continuously be considering how technology can help the business perform better, be more efficient or enable its people to focus on more income-generating and income-producing aspects of the business. Too often the "expense" of technology clouds an owner's perception about what technology can do for the business in the long run. Take a step back and consider how technology may be a solution that gives you and your people more time to market or enhances your marketing through greater efficiencies.

Physical location: Being home-based saves on overhead expenses and can be an excellent tax write-off. This can enable you to invest dollars in other areas that make more sense. An office presence however, can be a smart investment too. If you need space to present the appropriate image or to accommodate workers or meetings with clients, you may need to consider a location outside your home. Later, as your business grows and continues to expand in a rented space, a mortgage might become a better alternative. The property would be an investment and a tangible asset for both the business and you. The key is to understand how your physical location plays into your company image, your operations and your customer service. All three aspects need to be considered to make an effective decision.

Quick Moves

A custom home builder was in the midst of expanding with an impressive stand-alone commercial office and showroom. They were still several months from completion when his current leased space was up for renewal. With no option to go month-to-month, the owner leased a temporary, low-rent warehouse unit to curtail expenses until his new space was ready to be occupied. Shortly afterwards, rumors spread that his business was in trouble. A consultant helped him quickly realize that his expense mentality was the culprit, so the owner made two critical changes that set the record straight. He invested in "Under Construction" signage to make passers-by on the busy highway aware of his new facility. He then moved from the low-rent warehouse space into one of his spec homes, temporarily transforming the garage into a complete office and showroom welcome center. These quick moves immediately squelched the rumors and brought positive attention to the company's expansion.

Hiring: Making those first hires is one of the toughest hurdles for many business owners to get over. That's the result of viewing the position as an overhead expense rather than as an investment. You need to factor your time into the equation. Before the first hire, the business owner's time is typically monopolized by necessary but non-income-generating activities. An additional person is needed because the business owner is devoting too much time to these activities. It makes more sense to put someone else in charge of the tasks. The bottom line is that in order to grow beyond the place where the business is currently, hiring is necessary. If no one is available to do what needs to be done, it won't get done.

Well Interpreted Plan

Co-owners of a language services company were feeling the pinch of the economy as contracts began being delayed and then indefinitely put on hold. The company's growth

plan was set for hiring a key administrative position to
support the owners in the upcoming fiscal year. With the
economy affecting sales, it became even more imperative
for one of the owners to be able to target and market the
business more aggressively while the other owner oversaw
the work and kept it moving for clients. The owners
determined that hiring an administrative assistant was
critical for this to happen. By having a clear strategy and
understanding that the new position was an investment
that played into their well thought-out plan, the firm
continued to realize double-digit growth as the owners
were able to devote their time to the best possible uses.

Not clear on how to assess an expense to determine if it is an investment? Use these statements to help you identify a justifiable investment. If you can answer yes to one or more of these, what you are considering is an investment, not an expense.

Measurement:
- Can be directly measured for increased productivity
- Can be directly measured for greater efficiencies in a process
- Can be directly measured for increased profitability
- Can be directly measured for increased sales in business
- Can recoup and realize a financial gain as a result of the monies spent

Enhancements:
- Will allow time for income-generating or income-producing activities
- Will improve individual, team or customer service performance
- Will enhance, reinforce or protect the company image
- Will add credibility or capability that can be promoted
- Will aid in distinguishing the company against competitors

Make it your business to explore and analyze each expense with an investment mentality. Not only will it help you make better decisions, it could also put you ahead of the curve while others are cutting expenses and forgetting about investing in their businesses altogether.

Beyond the Green

Two commercial construction company owners
determined even before opening their business that they
were in a service business, not just a building business.
By offering top-level accessibility and open

communications at all levels of the company, clients were treated as top priority and handled with the care and attention of a friend or family member. The goal at the end of each and every project was that the client not only liked their building, but also enjoyed doing business with the company. The owners instilled this mentality throughout the organization, knowing that the earned trust would result in repeat projects and enthusiastic references to others considering the firm. This approach included investing in staff tradesmen and craftsman with the ability to self-perform portions of the work instead of using subcontractors. They were a service-driven, customer-centric construction firm, not a general contractor, and were proud of it. They wanted to assure total quality, not just profess it. Their commitment to investing in quality and service was further exemplified when the green wave of sustainability hit the Carolinas where their company was based. Seeing an opportunity where others saw dollar signs, they focused on being a true partner with their clients in gaining LEED certifications for the projects. It was the attention to details that earned their reputation and, therefore it was not a value-added afterthought. Established in 2001, the company continues to realize 25 percent annual growth and is ranked the top Green Builder in Charlotte, NC, #10 in North Carolina, and 70th in the nation by Engineering News and Record. It just goes to show that when you see beyond the green, you make plenty of friends, connections, and profits that carry you up, up and away from the pack.

•   •   •

Once you make the commitment to understand and know the difference between an expense and an investment, you can be among those businesses that not only survive but thrive, whatever the economic climate.

10
Repackaged & Delivered

Does it feel as though the marketplace has decided your products or services are no longer needed? Are you struggling and scrambling to get whatever comes through the door to make ends meet?

The first thing you need to do is stop. NOW. Take a step back to look at your business, your marketplace and where there are still opportunities. Before you give up, get strategic. Some of the most ingenious ideas and innovations have occurred when times were tough and businesses needed to be scrappy to be happy. While looking at ways to be more efficient or effective, they discovered opportunities that helped them view their existing products, services and processes with sharper vision. They not only learned why customers weren't buying, but also what they would buy and why.

Growth companies often introduce new products in a down market because they understand that during these times something new is appealing and also inspires hope that things are about to turn around. They literally help shift the market mindset from doom-and-gloom to cope-and-hope. These companies also know that although their customers have less money to spend, they will spend it on an offering that is different while addressing a real need.

You don't need an entire research and development department dedicated to introducing new products or services. Some of the savviest business owners have looked at their existing offerings and repackaged them in ways that appeal to different markets or better serve their existing ones.

Repackaged Products: Creating value for customers is something every company should be doing all the time. All too often, it is only when times get tough that a company analyzes the true value of its products and services for the customers. One action to consider is offering a group of products for a packaged price for a limited time period. This instills urgency while also helping you reduce inventory that would otherwise be sitting there. You can also take a low-cost product and offer it as a value-added free bonus item to a higher margin product. The key is to put together what makes sense to the buyer and not just what you have sitting on the floor and are trying to unload. If you are a manufacturer, another opportunity that exists is in scrutinizing what is being done with the scrap, leftovers and remnants. You could be throwing profits or a product idea away and not even know it. Is there a way to use the scrap, remnants or leftovers to provide a new offering to an entirely new market segment or to your existing market segment?

Prime Time Cuts

When a specialty producer of all-natural poultry and game began to see the economy taking another turn downward, its second-generation owner and his leadership team knew from experience that the key to staying ahead of the curve was to stay in tune with what was most important and valuable to its market. Being true to the company's mantra that if "everyone else is doing it, we won't," the team continually puts focused creativity and innovation on their cutting board with sustainable and enviable results. Over several decades the company had built an impressive reputation with the finest restaurants and gourmet retail markets across the country. In 2001, it sold its distribution and commodity business to entirely focus on specialty production, because there was no-one bringing exquisite poultry and game products to market in the manner demanded by chefs and culinary aficionados. Previous experience had proven that bringing something new to the finest tables would bring growth during downtrodden times. True to form, the company introduced an Epicure Reserve® product line, representing its most expensive offering at that time, which resulted in a 15 percent increase in sales. It also secured the exclusive rights to offer Poulet Rouge Fermier, a Label Rouge chicken from France. Because its poultry and small game were considered among the finest due to its meticulous care and attention to old

> **Commerce never stops entirely. This is the one time you can use the word "never" and it is accurate. Barring an apocalypse, commerce is simply the way of the world. *Business* may not be transacting at breakneck pace, but it is still occurring. There is always an opportunity for your business, if you are willing to see it.**

world process, making use of every part was considered a culinary challenge as well as smart business. Portion control is important in delivering product to restaurants, resulting in trimmings that other producers would toss. This company's chef welcomed the opportunity by creating an entire line of hors d'oeuvres made from trimmings and by-products including petite wings, rumaki, and kabobs. The company's varieties of chicken sausage with flavors such as blueberry and maple or chipotle pepper continue to receive rave reviews and national attention. By continuing to offer what no one else does in quite the same way, this company proves that demand can stay steady even in challenging times.

Repackaged Services: During the economic downturn that occurred after 9-11, service industries were hit hard, including travel, information technology consulting, training and development, marketing and advertising, and staffing. This is holding true in today's economy as well. In most cases, the biggest cut-backs are being made by large companies on the business-to-business front. Small businesses relying on their large business deals were caught in a quagmire of contracts put on hold or cancelled. Cash flow became virtually nonexistent. Consumer-based businesses took a hit from high-end buyers who held their investments close to their vests in anticipation of more stock market plunges.

However, while many businesses were retreating, other businesses began looking where cut-backs were less drastic. For business-to-business companies, these were in the mid-market and even small business sectors. Another sector spending was the government. The government increases spending during downturns. Some scratch their heads wondering where this money is coming from given the deficit, but opportunity is opportunity. Commercial construction companies and architectural firms that focus on sustainability and green technology have been kept busy with government opportunities because they offered this expertise when their competitors did not. Technology, training and staffing companies shifted their focus so they could be of better service to government or small and medium-sized businesses. Consumer service companies from restaurants to automotive care offered ways for middle-income and upper-income families to get more for less.

Repackaged Delivery: Is there a way you can repackage the way you deliver your products or services to make them more appealing to your target market? A trend that occurs in economically challenging times is a phenomenon called cocooning. Basically, consumers are opting to stay home more and entertain themselves more at home. Restaurants offering to-go family sized packaged dinners are an example of leveraging this concept.

Maid to Order

*A maid service offered a special pricing program for
monthly heavy cleaning of only the bathrooms and
kitchens in the home. These are the areas in the home
where the most grime typically accumulates and where
busy households would value getting help. The service
also included a special offer on a first come, first serve
basis for Saturdays. That's when a family would
normally be doing the cleaning themselves. For added
interest, the company threw in a special cross
promotional offer for a family morning outing. While
the service did the deep cleaning, the family enjoyed some
quality time away. When the families returned with
smiles on their faces, they were greeted by a clean kitchen
and bathrooms. Not only did the service get new clients
who had not previously used a maid service, but when
times picked up economically, they were able to increase
their frequency with clients who valued the service and
wanted the maid team in more often.*

• • •

Take yourself back to when you first started your business. Chances are you
were inspired with an idea to repackage the way an existing business was
providing its services or products. Now you simply need to take that same
impassioned mindset and put it to work on your own products and services for
profit-generating results.

11
Productizing Expertise

In these tough times, entrepreneurs are seeking new ways to create sales while not losing sight of their core competencies and business model. Often, what made a business model strong is now a source of frustration as ideal markets put projects on hold and delay contracts indefinitely. As an entrepreneur, you are probably the brain or master technician behind the capabilities you provide. That means the pressure is on you as your staff looks to you to get your business out of its funk and into another level of growth and prosperity.

Savvy business owners take advantage of this lull in business to gear up in ways that will recession-proof and "owner-proof" the business. What this means is taking measures to leverage the expertise of the owner in ways that bring money into the business via new target markets in new ways. Done properly, this also creates a stream of value that is appealing when the owner sells or doesn't want to be physically present to keep sales coming in.

Is it time for you to "productize" your expertise and create profit-generating products? Known as an "infopreneur," this new kind of business owner is leveraging every aspect of the information age and putting an entrepreneurial spin on it to become successful. Chances are you already have pieces in place to easily create some of these products. Here are some options to consider.

From Research to eReport: White papers, case studies and research that demonstrate your knowledge and insight are excellent ways to produce eReports or bulletins that others in your industry or target market will be willing to pay for. Consider conducting timely research that addresses a current challenge and then publishing a report of your findings. Already have a white paper? Consider offering it as an eReport with updated information and insight.

From Process to Packaged System: Those who cannot afford your services or hourly rates can often afford a do-it-yourself system. It allows you to serve a target market that, although not ideal for your core services, is perfect for a packaged system. An infopreneur understands this and reaches a new target market by taking their business's unique process or approach and putting it into a packaged system that can help someone utilize it on their own.

From Consultant to Trainer: As a consultant, there is a training aspect in what you do that can translate nicely into a program for newcomers in your industry or be a means of offering your expertise to a market that can't afford your consulting fees. This latter group might be interested in attending a training program to learn from your knowledge and expertise. My business launched a training division in 2004 to serve start-up business owners who did not have the budget for a marketing firm. They have become some of our best referral sources for our consulting business even though they only use our training offerings. With the Internet, cutting-edge infopreneurs are using teleseminars and webinars to eliminate the overhead of a physical facility while offering greater convenience to their markets.

Booked Solid

How did a yoga instructor, martial arts master and actor evolve into a multi-million dollar author, speaker and entrepreneur? He did it the smart way: by studying the principles of success, documenting these success principles and then sharing his story with the world as a business coach and infopreneur extraordinaire. From his first published book to several best-sellers afterwards, he leveraged his know-how with a meticulously orchestrated business system, spin-off products and programs. This demonstrated he not only practiced what he preached, but was willing to share how to do it with others. Combining tactical relevancy with emotionally-charged motivation and inspiration, he established a university platform, a certified coaching program and an online community of big thinkers. Today, he is a regular contributor to the New York Times, Inc. Magazine, Entrepreneur, The Wall Street Journal, Boston Globe, CNBC and MSNBC. Most impressive of all is how he has spawned other multi-million dollar success stories by

> *Productizing one's expertise not only offers a source of revenue when companies can't afford consultants, but also provides a form of residual income that does not require your physical presence. This can eventually become your means of retirement.*

people following his example and teachings. He proudly
considers those he has helped create their own success as
the true measure of his legacy and worth as an
entrepreneur.

From Expert to Author: While it may seem like a daunting task, a book offers instant credibility and a wealth of product opportunities. Interest and demand for spin-off products can provide a built-in buying group that offers valuable suggestions and waits anxiously to purchase your next offering.

From Purpose to Podium: Public speaking is often a strategic public relations initiative. Although you are not paid to share your expertise, you do get free exposure. However, once you gain a reputation and a following, you can begin charging fees to those who want to hear you speak in person. The best speakers are ones who not only share their knowledge, but also speak with passion and conviction. Let your enthusiasm show through, and you could open up a speaking career that also opens up immense back-room sales opportunities for your products.

From Being Seen to Being Heard: Learning while on the go is a thriving industry that began in the 1990s. For people of all ages, listening to information and audio presentations on the car DVD player or downloading them to an iPod or other MP3 device is a common and popular way to learn and get information. What do you have in your arsenal that is worth hearing?

•　　　•　　　•

To inspire the infopreneur in you, take a look at what you already have that could be adapted and turned into a product in one of these categories. Start with one product or offering and go from there. When you start to see money going into your bank account as if by magic, you will be glad you took the first step.

12

Systemized Marketing

If you have ever caught yourself saying you really need to get out and market your business, you clearly have not made marketing an operational aspect of your business. Marketing is not something you do only when you think you need it. It is something you do every day as a part of your business operations.

I know what you are thinking. You don't have enough hours in the day to do marketing in addition to providing services, making products and running your company. I am sympathetic to your situation. While you may not have enough time now, you could gain some time back and get more done by systemizing your marketing as well as some of your operations.

Growth companies understand that marketing is as much a part of their operational day-to-day activity as the services and products being provided and produced.

Customer Relationship Management Systems (CRM): Effectively managing communications and interaction with customers and prospects will set you apart from most competitors. Business communications are in dismal shape. Although it is complex, the communications highway represents a huge opportunity to set your company apart. CRM helps systemize your communications and serves as a catalyst for nurturing communications and capturing critical information about your customers and prospects. Programs such as Outlook, Access or ACT can also be used to systemize your communications. If you or your marketing team gets easily sidetracked by day-to-day concerns, these programs can issue alerts so you don't forget a planned communication or follow-up. Allow technology to help you communicate better and more consistently with your customers.

Internal Communications: Part of effectively serving and staying on top of customer needs is in having a strong system of communications internally within your company. If customers are beginning to say you or others in your company are more difficult to reach, the reality is that information or answers they are seeking are difficult to get. If they had called and someone else had been able to give them the answer, then the fact that you or the other person was not available would have been a non-issue. This issue was one that I had to address in my own company. As a result, we established three different documentation and status protocols in my company to alleviate this concern. Getting answers and updates is critical to customer service — empowering your entire organization with the ability to respond through systems and procedures will give you an edge.

Inside Out

The founder of an optical engineering and systems integration company knew all too well how effective properly integrated systems and processes generated results for its aerospace, defense and medical clients. Therefore, it was only logical to take the same approach in its marketing efforts. One goal was locking up long-term contracts by pursuing $8-million-plus jobs rather than smaller ones that typically required the same level of effort. At the core of their marketing process was an emphasis on communications, starting from the inside out. Internal communications at all levels was conducted like clockwork to assure seamless efforts in completing client projects and pursuing opportunities. Fifteen-minute huddles where salespeople provided one-minute summaries via GoToMeeting kicked off each day. Weekly 60-minute priority-watch meetings were conducted to keep everyone on track. Monthly three-hour tactical meetings focused on resolving any big issues or to share resources. Bi-monthly updates from the president gave everyone a top-down view of the company and its markets. Quarterly Tiger Team strategy meetings assembled a group of employees from all levels of the company with a session leader to solve a particular challenge or to look ahead to anticipate opportunities. A

> **Growth companies understand that marketing is as essential to their business as breathing is to living. No one worries about their breathing stopping. Why? Because our respiratory system operates without us having to think about it. The same holds true when you have systems in place in your business.**

CRM system was implemented to assure ongoing and relevant contact with both customers and prospects. From online optimization and public relations efforts to trade shows and affiliations, all aspects of marketing were strategically linked together. They were also monitored for effectiveness as a means of building off one another or shifting where needed. To assure customer service on the technical side of the business, training was provided to help nurture and grow these soft skills in engineers and technicians. Through a focused strategy coupled with an intentional effort to make marketing an integral part of operations, this company realized 1300 percent growth from 2005 to 2009 and has booked 50 percent of its revenue commitments three to five years in advance.

Templates & Guides: Are there documents or communications that are used on a regular basis in your business? Anything – proposals, estimates, letters, reports and other communications – can be turned into templates to make preparing them easier and more efficient. I finally allowed my office manager to include style formatting in our analysis reports, strategies and plans. I was reluctant for the longest time and now don't even want to think about the time my staff and I wasted because we were doing things the hard way.

Discovery Forms & Processes: When someone calls your company, is there a formal way to capture information about the prospect before they are handed off to a salesperson or you? Sometimes an inquiry can be effectively qualified by the receptionist or whoever answers the phone. What are the initial key questions anyone can ask when someone calls? What information is critical to determine if this is a good prospect or needs to be referred to someone other than you?

Pricing & Estimating Systems: Is estimating a bottleneck in your business? Is your business pricing generic, or are there many factors to consider when determining pricing? Just because you offer customized solutions, doesn't mean your pricing cannot be systemized. Years ago I did an analysis of price ranges for our typical client projects. I began preparing proposals using these ranges, but also considered any variables I had identified. As a result, I have significantly minimized the time it takes to prepare a proposal with pricing.

Bidding Ado

A custom cabinetry business owner saw an explosion in the number of opportunities he received to submit bids to be a subcontractor for primary contractors serving *government construction projects. Even by working 16-hour days, he could not keep up with the demand of the estimating along with overseeing projects already underway. Numerous bid deadlines were missed, and he was beyond exhaustion. Although lamenting the $2,000 cost of an estimating software program, he realized it was an investment he needed to make. Not only did it enable him to estimate jobs at the click of a mouse, it also saved him time. This meant he could do other things, including having a "real" life. His business is successful at securing numerous bid contracts and he is able to more effectively focus on job delivery now that estimating is a snap.*

Inquiry and Submittal Systems: Typically, your website is the first place most people will visit before calling you. Do you make it easy to submit an inquiry online? Does your inquiry form give you some added insight so you can respond better? Do you answer typical customer questions (FAQs) on your website? When someone calls the business, are your office hours and website shared in an on-hold message or voicemail greeting? In your voicemail greeting, are callers directed where they need to go with ease? Are they always given the option of speaking to a real person so they are not trapped in "voicemail hell"? Do you have a standard for when calls or web-based inquiries will receive a response?

Tracking & Response Systems: How are you managing the flow of production for products or work performed? Do you have a system so anyone in your company can check the status of an order or project even if they are not working on it? Do you have a means for customers to track their order if it is important for them?

•   •   •

One of the biggest deterrents for putting new systems in place is the belief that time cannot be spared to install and implement them. Another deterrent is that the information needed to establish a system, document, process or procedure is in the owner's head, and you never have the time share it. But if any of these could create some efficiencies in your organization or take some pressure off you, isn't it worth the time to do it?

CUSTOMER RELATIONS

13
Masters of Mindshare

All too often, when I ask business owners to describe their ideal target customer, they rattle off figures about income and geography. While it is important to know the demographics and geographics of your customer base to make better marketing decisions, understanding the psychology, or psychographics, of your ideal customer is the key to making good strategic decisions. Whenever I take business owners through the exercise of getting inside the heads of their customers, there are always numerous "aha" moments. This more in-depth understanding not only helps them make more strategic decisions, but also helps them know how to better communicate and attract the right customers. It also helps keep away those who are not ideal.

I often tell business owners they need to know their target market like the FBI tries to know a serial killer. Some might think I am joking, but I am dead serious. High-growth companies get this with the growth numbers to prove it. They know their customers intimately, and they constantly focus on getting to know them better. They understand it is better to segment customers based on how they think. You need to start thinking this way too.

Who is NOT ideal and why? This is one of the first things you need to answer about your ideal market. Why? Because the key to effective marketing and communications is to attract those who are most ideal as customers of your business, while communicating in a way that also discourages those that are not ideal from inquiring. When you communicate from a true knowledge base about your customer, you will also help those less ideal prospects eliminate themselves because they don't think or approach things in quite the same way. Therefore, your time and energy is spent on those who are most likely to do business with you and who appreciate what you have to offer. Too many businesses spend far too much time trying to convince people to do business with them. If you are spending time convincing, then you are very likely not clear on who your ideal and not ideal customers are. Consider those customers who have not been ideal in the past? Why is this? What attitudes, values or approach in working with you were not appealing about them?

Wayward Customers: Just because business has slowed and you should be grateful for the business you do have does not mean that you should take any and all customers. Many businesses get themselves in a rut during tough times by forgetting who they best serve. As a result, they get caught in a quagmire of trying to keep customers happy that are not ideal, who are not making them money, and who are keeping them from effectively serving those customers who are ideal and profitable. Take stock in your customer base and graciously hand off or refer those who are not ideal.

Not Created Equal

A landscape architect hired a marketing consultant after becoming frustrated with "tire kickers" coming to his firm to price-shop his services. When asked to describe his ideal customer, he quickly answered, "People with a home worth $500,000 or more located on at least a half-acre site." The consultant pointed out two half-million dollar homes were not created equal once the psychographics of their owners was considered. One home was constructed in a track-housing community with six home plan selections. These homeowners contacted him when they realized their home looked like another one a block away. However, they ended up going back to select the landscaping package offered with their home because of the lower price. The other home was built in a custom-home community. It was a unique property with owners who appreciated professional services offering originality. The landscaping needed this kind of touch, too. They considered everything they owned as an expression of who they were, and image was of utmost importance. They worked in high-profile positions and socialized in high-profile ways, attending fundraisers and cultural events and supporting the arts. Once he recognized the differences in these two types of homeowners, the architect realized he had been causing

> **High-growth companies know their ideal target market like the FBI knows the style, personality, motivators, and thinking of a serial killer. They know what is on their customers' minds so well that the ideal ones keep knocking on the door and those who are not ideal never come knocking.**

his own headaches by sending direct mailings to track-home communities. He shifted to mailing exclusively to custom communities. He also became the only landscape architecture to run ads in programs for the symphony, children's theater and other performing arts. Now the prospects attracted to his business are ideal and know his firm is ideal for them.

Lifestyle & Work Style: There are several key factors you need to determine about your ideal customer. Who else do they turn to for guidance, support, advice or services? These resources can be great referral sources or cross-promotional partners. What organizations are your ideal target customers involved in, personally and professionally? How can you help them live better or do their job better? How can you help them serve their customers or family better? What is their corporate culture like? What is their lifestyle? How can you help them serve their employees better? What activities are they involved in on a regular basis? Who else influences their decisions and how? What do they read on a regular basis? What do they do for entertainment? How do they view money, both in terms of spending it and acquiring it? How do they view money as it relates to work and to life and how they spend it? Create a list of anything reflective of the work or lifestyle of your ideal market. You will be surprised how much it inspires your marketing decisions.

Money, Money, Money

A Pilates studio owner hired a consultant to help plan the opening of a second location. When the consultant asked her to describe her ideal target market, the owner responded with "women aged 35 to 65 with disposable income." After the owner added a few other demographic and geographic characteristics, the consultant asked how the studio's clients viewed money. The owner had never really thought about it before. As the discussion continued, the consultant helped her realize she had three ideal client profiles with three different money mindsets: Old Money, New Money and Corporate Money. The studio was located in a college town where doctors and lawyers received their undergraduate degrees. A majority of the clients coming from this community were Old Money clients who enjoyed theater performances and symphony on the college green, supported the college sports teams and volunteered for organizations such as cultural arts groups and Habitat for Humanity. Some of these women worked and some did not. They tended to be older, to be health-conscious and active in gardening, hiking, tennis and enjoying their children and grandchildren. They did Pilates to be stronger, have more energy and to ultimately live a long and healthy life. The New Money clients were slightly younger and lived outside the college town in nearby suburbia. These women were wives of sports figures and executives living the country-club life. They did Pilates because they wanted to look young, sophisticated and glamorous, as if they were someone you'd see walking on the red carpet of a Hollywood premiere. The Corporate Money clients were professional women who typically attended classes early in the morning or just after work. The main reason they did Pilates was to help them deal with the stress of their hectic lifestyles. It was an escape that helped relieve the pressures and demands of their jobs. With this new understanding of the three distinct segments within the same age, gender, and income range, the Pilates studio owner realized the importance of marketing to these women in different ways. This insight further confirmed that the second location she was considering was ideal for the New Money mindset. The second location opened successfully while the first location continued to grow, all because of understanding how an individual's mindset about money plays a role in his or her life.

Psychographics: What weighs heaviest on your ideal customers' minds and causes them to lose sleep? What is most important to them and why? What could they care less about? What are their unanswered questions/unresolved issues that you could address? What are they most knowledgeable about? In what areas are they least knowledgeable? What values do you share? How are you like them? How are you what they would like to be? How can you help them become more like they want to be? How can you help them be better at something, achieve something, know more about something, improve their circumstances, or get more for their money? What incorrect assumptions do they make about your business? What things do they need to know that relate to your business?

More Equals Less

*The owner of a comprehensive benefits company realized
early on that the key to differentiating his company was
in the details and the bottom-line for his clients. So his
company focused on increasing and restoring profits for
his clients through value-driven, wellness-focused
benefits programs rather than price cutting. While
competitors approached prospects with a focus on lower-
priced options, this owner knew the lowest price does not
necessarily equate to long-term higher profits. Prices
inevitably increase at the annual renewal, meaning the
only recourse for those focusing solely on costs is to cut
employee benefits. Another reason for rising insurance
premiums is increasing claims. Without managing and
reducing them, a company can't expect to effectively
minimize increases. And if claims are out of control,
chances are workers are less productive. This insurance
specialist knew the best way to serve clients was not about
offering a lower-priced premium. It was about providing
a solutions-based benefits plan that enabled a company
to effectively manage and monitor its healthcare costs
and employee claims. Critical to this agency's success
was educating and assisting clients in incorporating
health and wellness-driven initiatives so claims
decreased. This meant encouraging and offering
incentives to workers to make healthier, more cost-
effective decisions. Of special note was the way this
agency approached employees' chronic health conditions.
While other companies used pre-existing conditions as a
reason for higher premiums, this agency helped clients
educate employees to better manage their conditions so
they made healthier decisions. For instance, through
wellness education and incentives, a diabetic patient was
able to reduce annual claims costs to $1,800 compared to
the average annual claims for diabetics of $18,000.
Multiply this type of claim reduction company-wide,
and the client's company was able to earn a premium
reduction without cutting benefits. While competitors are
happy with a 10 percent closure rate based on price-
cutting alone, this agency boasts a 75 percent qualified*

closure rate and an industry-leading retention rate. With
annual double-digit growth and being rated among the
top-performing agencies in the country, this company
proves that doing more equals less in a very profitable
way.

•   •   •

There are many other questions you can ask, but the ones posed in this secret will get you started. Understanding the mentality and emotional makeup of your customer will do more than increase your confidence in serving them. It will also increase your advantage over your competitors, as they focus on their markets' demographics and geography only. Best of all, you will be using your available resources more wisely by attracting ideal customers to your business, an important bottom-line benefit, especially during these challenging times.

14

Relationships vs. Transactions

When times are tough, and sales are not coming in as steadily and easily as they once were, many business owners sabotage their sales efforts. They are trapped in a transaction mindset when their marketing efforts should be focusing on building relationships. Often, one of the reasons for their slowing sales is because transactions – the need for them or the fear of their lack – has shifted their focus to making the sale instead of earning and appreciating it. Have you fallen into this way of thinking?

When you are in a transaction mindset, you get caught up in inking the deal rather than building a relationship. High-growth companies understand this and never forget that a lifelong relationship is always the goal – not a quick sale. Notice I said a lifelong *relationship*, not a lifelong *customer*. It is vital to view all your company's interactions – with employees, vendors and customers – as relationships to be nurtured.

Even if your business model does not call for creating lifelong customers (you might reconsider this, though), taking care of customers is still of paramount importance. Making sure customers have a positive, memorable experience motivates them to encourage others to patronize your business. That creates a lifetime of referrals even if they don't use your service again due to the nature of your business.

Goals: One of the first indicators that you may be caught in a transaction mindset is only focusing on the sales and profitability numbers versus how you are going to achieve them. If the only goals you have are increased percentages of sales and profits over last year, then you are in a transaction mindset. Take a look at your goals for the year. Your goals should go beyond dollars and include measurable benchmarks for how you expect to get these numbers. Do they include increases in the number of referrals from customers? Do they include any retention expectations based on sales from existing customers? Do they include increases in sales from new and existing customers through expanded capability areas or product offerings?

Now that your goals are more in alignment with building relationships versus making transactions, you now must look at how you are actually establishing and reinforcing your relationships.

Prospecting: Are cold calling and telemarketing primary activities in your marketing efforts? Then you are approaching generating new sales entirely from a transaction mindset. Think about telemarketing calls you have received yourself. Isn't the goal too often all about making that sale by the end of the call? And aside from the fact that the "Do Not Call" option for consumers makes telemarketing taboo for many businesses, is this really how you want your business to be viewed? Only about the sale? Cold calling makes the same impression. "You don't know me, but you should be buying from me." At the very least, you should have marketing and communications activity in place so that when you or someone representing your company makes a call to a prospect, it is a "warm" call because they have an idea of who you are, what you do, and why they should care to do business with you over a competitor or someone they may already be using now.

Before the Sale: When you are communicating with prospects, are you promoting your services and products before really understanding where their pain or needs might be? Before you can give answers, you need to get some answers. Never assume before confirming what is most needed and why. There is no better place to start than with existing customers. If you have added a product or capability, was it based on getting feedback from your customer base and are you first offering it to those who already know you before you go after prospects? I am simply amazed at how often I see businesses forgetting their existing or past customers when introducing something new in their business. Keep in mind that those who know you and like what you have done for them will be happy to share and encourage others to do business with you even if what you are offering as an addition is not a perfect fit for their needs right now.

> *High-growth companies do not consider cold calling or telemarketing primary marketing activities. This is true regardless of whether the companies relied on a commission-only or salary-based sales force. The focus is on building relationships.*

During the Sale: What are you doing once a sale has been made to keep the relationship top of mind? How are you showing your customer that having a relationship with them is valued and appreciated? How are you keeping them informed of progress and sharing insights or information that might benefit them while the service or product is being prepared or finalized?

360 Degrees of Respect

A niche securities bonds head trader could have viewed his operation like every other trading house, simply riding the wave of high returns and allowing transactions to be the company's guiding force. But the trader was savvy enough to know that to thrive, regardless of market conditions, relationships were at the core of each and every transaction. Acting on this principle was the key to his ongoing success. His mantra was "Give respect. Earn respect. Get respect." He first made it clear that his team of traders were first and foremost a team and not competing against each other. He structured incentives and bonuses around building their business collaboratively and supporting one another in all ways possible as millions of dollars of trades occurred daily. He insisted his traders buy securities targeted to specific needs with their clients' best interests in mind, so the transaction was a win-win for the firm and client. He put detailed systems in place with each team member overseeing and monitoring their responsibilities so transactions occurred accurately and seamlessly, thereby increasing the confidence of their growing list of clients. He dictated a proactive approach in working with both buyers and sellers with a conscientious effort to know them beyond the transaction. Personal phone calls were an everyday part of doing business, and face-to-face meetings were considered essential to continually increase clients' trust level. Asking questions and seeking to truly understand buyer or seller thresholds from both an institutional and personal level were considered the only way to conduct business. This has paid off with a dedicated loyal team in an industry where turnover is high. The bonds boutique has also realized continued growth every quarter since being established in 2001. While larger competitors are losing market share and market confidence, this "little engine that could," as the trader likes to call his team, proves that placing relationships over transactions results in win-win growth for everyone concerned.

After the Sale: Whether your business engages customers for an extended period of time or has a sales-and-completion cycle, you need to conscientiously maintain relationship-oriented interactions. This means implementing a communications program to stay in touch and proactively keep customers in the loop. What about prospects who haven't yet used your business? Qualified prospects should also be in your communications queue. Keeping them informed of what you have done for others turns into sales and a new relationship because they see you are making a difference for others on a regular basis. Giving them a taste of how you think and approach business gives them confidence that you value them beyond the sale.

•   •   •

What growth companies understand is that the key to ongoing sales is the follow-up and follow-through that creates a following. If you have perfected all three of these areas, you understand the powerful impact building relationships has on your sales, your bottom line and your place in the market – not just now, but also in the years to come.

15
Connecting Customers

Earning a customer's confidence to the point they refer you to others should always be a top priority for any business owner. But savvy business owners also look for ways to connect and refer their customers to one another as well as to others. What are you doing to connect your customers to each other? Think about it. They have many things in common, and you are a commonality that can bring them together. What are you doing to help connect them to other resources or support they might need?

A Common Cause: What common cause do your customers gravitate to and support? Can your business become a sponsor or hold a fundraising event to help the cause and connect customers in the process? Is there an activity or program you can put into place that will involve customers associated with the cause?

A Common Interest: The beauty of Secret #13 (truly getting to know your customers) is that it provides you with a base of information you can use to bring them together in unique ways — ways that your competitors are doing. What social or leisure activities do they enjoy? What hobbies or interests do they have in common, and how can this be an opportunity to bring them together?

People's Choice

When bank mergers were an everyday occurrence on the financial news front, a regional community bank stayed steadfast to its founding principles in being more about the people it served than the products it offered. Creating a connection with customers was of paramount importance to how this bank's leadership knew it would grow, simply by growing along with the communities it served. This meant calling a customer by their formal name initially and then first name after they had been in the bank a few times. It also meant recognizing and acknowledging the multiple employees of a business account and making a personal call when something did not appear right in the accounts. Unlike its competitors, representatives who just attended events and passed out cards, this bank truly became involved in the community. Identifying ways to bring customers together to interact and connect as a result of being customers of the bank was also important. For example, the bank began a travel club that offered a variety of excursions – half-day visits to a museum, day trips to the mountains or long journeys that took them to Europe or Africa. By offering it to a particular segment of its customer base, the bank brought value and the ability to know one's neighbors to a whole new level. Focus groups with customers or celebratory luncheon spreads for customer appreciation events at various branches continued to show that it is the people and the connections they make that create the greatest value over time. For this bank, it also reaped impressive growth, expanding from six branches in 1993 to 23 branches with more than $1 billion in assets. Best of all, it continues to realize growth while the financial and banking industry as a whole is in recovery, proving that when people take precedence over products, everyone wins.

> Eighty percent of high-growth companies in our study made it a practice to refer or connect customers with one another or other resources. They clearly understood that part of creating loyalty is helping customers make connections beyond what their business offers.

Cross Connections: Knowing your customers helps you better connect them on a one-to-one basis as well as in a group setting. For the consumer business, noting key interests and preferences can help you connect mothers seeking a particular activity for their children or alert a customer to an upcoming event other customers are raving about. If your market is business-to-business, you are in an ideal situation to refer your customers to one another. If you are in a niche where customers are in the same industry, you can sponsor a mastermind group or consortium to allow them to share best practices.

• • •

When customers feel connected, they stay connected. It becomes even more profound once you connect them with each other. Creating an environment where people feel valued and where sharing goes beyond checkbooks is an environment rich in loyalty.

16
Rewards vs. Incentives

Do you have a customer incentive program? If you do, then it is time to ask yourself why. If you don't have a customer incentives program in place, you won't have to break a bad habit and can start fresh with a better approach. What is wrong with offering an incentive program? If you feel you need to create incentives for customers to do business with you or to refer you business, you are not doing an effective job of serving them in the first place. The best way to get customer referrals is to wow them with your service, products, expertise and creativity and exceeding their expectations. Go to Secret # 21 to learn more about wowing customers.

Reward Referrals: Savvy business owners don't need an incentive program to gain referrals from customers. Their customers are already happily sending others their way, so no special incentive program is needed. However, showing appreciation for these referrals by rewarding customers for them is a common practice among growth companies.

Charitable Rewards

A high-end boutique that saw clients by appointment only knew its careful management of its executive and socialite clients' unique wardrobes was gaining attention. Clients were continually sharing the compliments they received from others wanting to know where they purchased their amazing suits, ensembles and accessories. As an incentive to encourage clients to refer new people, the boutique offered a $50 credit towards the referring client's next purchase. However, no new referrals came in as a result. Perplexed because of her clients' compliments, the boutique owner sought advice from a marketing consultant. The consultant helped the boutique owner realize that the $50 incentive was offered to a market that does not respond to discounts. With the *boutique's designer suits starting at $1,000 and the average client spending $3,000 or more per appointment, the $50 credit was simply not of value to them. Instead, the consultant recommended making a $50 charitable donation in the referring client's name as a thank you for their confidence and recommendation. This time the program was successful. Thousands of dollars have been donated to worthy causes as a result of the program and clients feel truly rewarded and appreciated.*

Reward Loyalty: Why is it that companies will offer all kinds of special promotions and gifts for people they don't know to win their business, but offer nothing to those who continue to do business with them? In most cases, these businesses are always chasing the sale because they are not taking care of and appreciating the customers they already have. Eventually, these customers move on to another business or service provider because they don't feel valued. Consider how you can reward your customers for their loyalty in meaningful ways.

Reward Multiple Purchases: There is a reason you see so many customer rewards programs. They work. Customers value them. What can you do to reward customers who regularly do business with you? What will be of value to them and set you apart? For example, a boutique selling resort and high-end sleepwear began giving customers special bonus items in conjunction with purchases over a certain amount. For instance, a customer could choose from a selection of jewelry items with a resort wear purchase of a specially formulated delicates wash for a sleepwear purchase.

> What is the difference between an incentive and a reward? An incentive is usually internally focused on the business and getting the customer to do something. A reward focuses on what is truly meaningful to the customer because the customer's loyalty is appreciated.

Reward Friends & Family: If your business is one where customers bring family and friends, recognize these natural connections with a specially-designed rewards program. One business tracked the sales of the referring customer's friends and family members. After sales reached a certain amount, the business hosted a special private gathering for the entire group.

Reward by Association: Are there common groups or organizations your customers are members of or are otherwise involved in? Offering a special reward to those who are members of a particular group is an excellent way to show your appreciation, plus gain additional customers from the same organization. Another meaningful gesture is to donate to the particular group's cause on behalf of your customers.

●　　●　　●

When you shift from an incentives mindset to a rewards mindset, you emphasize the importance of the relationship with your customer, not just their business. You show that exceeding their expectations is your standard way of doing business. You also show them you are not taking them for granted and are focused on earning their trust and loyalty on an ongoing basis.

17
Informing Customers

One of the best ways to show how much you value your customers is by keeping in touch with them. This transforms your business from one where they just make a transaction to one that sincerely wants to foster a relationship with them. Most importantly, it shows you genuinely care. Whether via e-mail, snail mail or a combination of the two, let your customers know you are thinking about them by informing and enriching them.

Newsletters or Bulletins: In spite of the plethora of mail everyone gets at work and at home, a publication done right can reap extensive benefits for a business by both informing and reinforcing what it brings to the market. The key to this kind of communication is to offer information and news that extends beyond your products and services and includes relevant nuggets of wisdom or tips that speak directly to your customers' interests and concerns. Put insight-filled information front-and-center while also including any promotion of your company secondary. The best publications are quick-reads that can be easily digested. You know you have a winner when it is kept, shared and anticipated!

Focused Insight

A small business operations and process consultant was determined to communicate to her database differently than anything she had seen before. With 20 years of experience as a manager in Corporate America, she realized that small business owners were a different breed of managers. She also knew that to be of value to the business owner, she needed to be not just an advisor. Offering tools and a means for the business owner to assess their current situation would be non-threatening while also inspiring them to take action to work with her to solve a particular challenge. With her focus being on helping fast-growth companies survive the pitfalls of success, the idea of a focused one-page bulletin was formulated. A quick read in a storytelling format, the bulletin sought to enable business owners and their management team the ability to assess how they were doing operationally in a particular focus area by a simple scalable point system. The first issue was mailed three years after the firm had opened its doors. The bulletins became so popular and anticipated that the list continued to grow as referral contacts and the business community as a whole valued these bulletins for their succinct insight-generating ability. Now celebrating its 15th year in business, the consultant has gained marketplace positioning as the expert in operational growth of a company. Her bulletins have also caught the attention of media who have published them. While issues are also available in email format and are listed on the company website, the bulletin is still being mailed with 70 percent of the company's mailing list preferring a hard copy so they can keep it on file and reread or share with others. Even with the electronic world we are now in, the value of a paper with a wealth of information and insight is still enjoyed the old-fashioned way.

> Based on interviews with thousands of customers of small business, more than half of customers were aware of LESS than 50 percent of what a business offers. During my 26 years in business, I have only found a handful of companies that effectively inform customers about their capabilities and products.

eZines or eBulletins: E-mail-based communication is an inexpensive and powerful way to stay in touch, inform and inspire. But be sure it is formatted to work as an HTML within your e-mail and not attached as a PDF. When you attach it rather than embed it, chances are it will land in people's spam or junk folders or be rejected altogether. There are numerous cost-effective programs to help you affordably and easily produce your electronic communications including Constant Contact and iContact.

New Products or Services: Whenever you have a new product or service, your existing customer base should be the first to receive the announcement. Even if the product is targeting a new or slightly different audience, never underestimate your existing customers' circles of influence. You are sharing the information as much to inform them as you are hoping they will inform others. I am amazed by the number of times I have seen businesses send out elaborate mailings announcing a new product or service to a purchased list but not send it to its current database.

Near Miss

A producer of several grades of alumina powder used in everything from fluorescent lighting to computer disks hired a firm to interview their customers' purchasing agents and decision-makers for feedback as they prepared to expand. When the interviewer asked about awareness of the company's various capabilities and products, a large and long-time customer was surprised to learn the company offered the newest finest grade concentration powder. He told the interviewer he was just about to award a contract for this kind of product. After the interview was over, the purchasing agent gave permission for the interviewer to share the information with the manufacturer as he wanted to include the company in the bidding process. When the marketing company contacted the division president to share the news, he was outraged that the customer did not know about the product as they had just sent out an announcement about it. Further research revealed that the mailing went to a purchased list of targeted prospects, but was not mailed to the customer base. The company ended up getting the contract, and a new protocol for keeping customers informed was established.

Announcements & News: When sending news announcements to the media or posting them to your website, alert your customer base, too. There is a sense of privilege that comes with knowing news before it hits the general media or goes online. When a customer later reads about your accomplishment or development, they can smile knowing they were privy to it before others.

Status Updates & Alerts: If your company is going through any major transition, sending periodic updates or alerts about any interruption in service or schedule is not only appreciated, but demonstrates proactive consideration to your customers. If you keep a pulse on industry or market factors of value to your customers, sending alerts or breaking news about developments that could impact them will set you apart from the competition.

•　　•　　•

It takes much less energy to sell to those already using your products or services. Yet the major reason customers change providers is that someone else establishes stronger communications, connections and values them. Customers view a company that stays in touch as one that cares and wants their business more. When you make communications part of how you relate to your customers on a regular basis, you reinforce their decision to do business with you. There is a sense of pride that comes with knowing more and feeling part of an inner circle.

18

The Personal Touch

Letting those associated with your business know how much you appreciate their role in your success is something you can never do too much or too often. This is as true for your employees, vendors and suppliers as it is for your customers. Particularly in a down economy, nothing should be taken for granted, especially the relationships that help make your business continue to operate.

Being Attentive & Focused: How attentive are you to your customers' needs when you meet with them or they walk in the door? How truly present are you? What standards have you set for how your employees serve, relate to and take care of customers? Common courtesy alone can go a long way toward making customers feel welcomed, appreciated and valued.

Just For You

An aspiring salon owner had a vision: to bring a quality salon and spa to a small lake community. Residents were going to nearby towns for pampering spa treatments. The demographics and appeal were ideal to bring a true spa experience to the area. In her initial research, she determined to start off cautiously by offering manicures and pedicures. The immediate area competitors approached manicures and pedicures as an in-and-out quick convenience versus a relaxing experience. TVs were blaring and people were lined up in stations to be served until the next person came in. She opened her boutique in 2006 with a luxury salon feel and atmosphere, complete with complimentary glasses of wine, feng shui décor, and basic-to-deluxe pampering manicure and pedicure treatments. She made it a point to get to know each customer, keeping records and notes so each time they came in, they would be remembered and were made to feel special. She and her staff continuously sought to know what else clients would be interested in and added services accordingly. Birthdays and celebrations were noted. Group gatherings were encouraged for mothers and daughters, office personnel, birthdays, holidays, anniversaries, and special events like prom. Sunday hours were added to the delight of clients, resulting in a 25 percent increase in sales. In spite of an economic downturn, by 2009 the salon had grown to a full-service salon and spa offering hair care, professional make up, massages, facials, tanning, manicures and pedicures. Ask the salon owner her secret to successful double-digit annual growth and she will say it is their personal touch from the very beginning. For her, it is more than satisfying the client. It is also about showing the client how much you really care and that they are why you are in business.

Handwritten Notes: Think about the last time you received a handwritten note. You kept it, didn't you? What was once the standard way to communicate has gone by the wayside, replaced by e-mails and phone calls. But a personalized handwritten note says a lot more than the actual words. It says someone took the time to send a greeting, thank you or acknowledgement because they deemed you were special and worth the effort. Yet it really doesn't take all that much time, especially if you have a system in place. One company, Send Out Cards, has been successful by converting this concept into an easy, customizable system that has made sending cards with a personal touch easy to do on a regular basis.

> One of the best things you can do for your business is to outline in detail the experience and feelings you want your customers to walk away with and how you will accomplish this. The personal touches you incorporate into this process are priceless and will not only impress customers, but win them over for life.

Acknowledging by Name: Do you expect everyone in your company to know customers by name and then use their names when greeting them? Does everyone in your company greet and acknowledge your customers in a way that makes them feel appreciated? A bond is created when someone takes the time to know your name, so make this a component of what sets your business apart. A personal greeting is a powerful reminder that the customer is a person and not just someone who makes purchases at your business.

Common Interests & Values: Acknowledging your customers' interests adds a personal touch that tells them they are valued individuals. A company that alerts customers to events of interest to them is viewed as one that values their customers. High-growth companies also understand the power of posting and proudly proclaiming their corporate values because they know these values are also shared by their ideal customers.

All vs. Only You: Make sure you are not the only person in your company expressing your appreciation to customers, vendors and suppliers. Hearing from various people in your company throughout the year saying "Thank you!" or "Way to go!" will be meaningful and impactful every time a customer receives one. It also expands the company beyond you and demonstrates you have a hard-working team working to serve the customer.

Snail Mail vs. E-mail: Don't be quick to always use e-mail because of its convenience. Junk filters and inundated inboxes can cause your communication to be lost or missed. Your customers have communication preferences and should be communicated with in the way they prefer. A training and development company snail-mailing a bi-monthly newsletter added an electronic e-mail version and asked recipients what format they preferred. More than 300 of the 500 recipients still wanted to get the newsletter by mail. A portion of them also wanted to receive an electronic version so they could easily forward it to others. The remainder of the database requested the electronic version only.

• • •

Knowing your entire staff personally cares about them and values their business should be an integral part of your customers' experience when they do business with you. Personal touches demonstrate that your appreciation of them is more than just words. Doing it in ways that is meaningful to them creates a loyalty that will envied by your competition.

19
Segmenting & Targeting

Commerce may slow down, but it never completely stops. This is the silver lining in this gray cloud called a recession. As a business owner, you have more power than you think. Now is the time to make the most out of current circumstances by using it as a catalyst to make your business even better through segmenting, targeting, focusing and prioritizing opportunities.

Targeting Customer Challenges: Don't let the current economic landscape make you think you have to cast your net wider to catch new customers. Now, more than ever, you should be focusing on who your ideal customer is. Secret #13 showed how you can do this by asking yourself who is not ideal and why. How well do you understand your customers' present mentality so you can hone in on what they still need in spite of scaling back? How have these times changed your target market's needs – and how can you meet them? How can you help your customers improve their current circumstance? How can you help them get more for their money?

Targeting Niches: There are five niche segments that can make your targeting and focusing efforts more lucrative.

- <u>Market Niche</u>: A market niche is defined by a common age grouping, such as Baby Boomers, Generation Y, or Millenniums. A market niche can also be defined by a common thread tying the segment together in business or in life, such as entrepreneurs or single parents. A mindset goes with each niche. This is why, as explained in Secret #13, the psychographics and work/life preferences of your ideal market are vitally important.

- <u>Industry Niche</u>: An industry niche is exactly what it says. It can be telecommunications, technology, healthcare, retail, industrial or banking/finance – the list goes on. The North American Industry Classification System (NAICS) and the Standard Industrial Classifications (SIC) both offer extensive listings of industry segments. Some businesses focus on segments within an industry niche, such as targeting only dental practices within the larger healthcare niche. To determine if focusing on a segment within an industry niche is a smart move for your business, assess your ability to serve it by using what you learned in Secret #5 and Secret #13.

- Cultural Niche: A cultural niche is based on an individual's ethnic heritage. Examples are African American, Hispanic and Asian-American. Understanding the customs and traditions of a cultural niche is vital to effectively marketing to them. Businesses have committed many numerous faux pas by jumping into a cultural niche without fully understanding it.

- Mentality Niche: Mentality niches have become more prominent in recent years as a target market focus. These can include spiritual, political or religious groupings. Notice I listed spiritual and religious separately? These are two different mentalities, so it is important to understand the nuances that differentiate them. There are segments within these niches as well. For instance, a business might target the Catholic or Jewish faith within the religious niche. Green and sustainable living is a relatively new mentality niche that is rapidly expanding.

> How can you take advantage of a down time? By looking at ways you can be more targeted, focused, profitable, and effective. This is also the time to rally your team and focus on ways to boost morale and get more done with less. Doing this on an ongoing basis is what makes good companies great and great companies growth companies.

- Lifestyle Niche: A lifestyle niche typically hones in on a group that participates in the same activity or hobby. For instance, those who travel extensively, are collectors or support the arts can be defined as lifestyle niches. Other examples are bicyclists, motorcyclists, hikers and gardeners.

Look at where your competitors are not focusing. Is there a particular niche within your ideal market that could set you apart as the go-to company to serve its members?

Mucho Gracias

A North Carolina community bank saw an opportunity when the 2000 census reported that the Hispanic market was a large and growing segment that needed to be served. Understanding the mentality of this market segment was critical to the banking industry adequately serving this population. The culture tended to mistrust large establishments even in their native lands. So an investigative team was assembled to study how to create a better banking experience and build trust with this growing population. The bank worked with the consulate, who, pleased to see a genuine interest in serving Hispanic residents, arranged for focus groups to share their fears, concerns and needs. Learning that many of them were unable to speak or read English, the bank began employing bilingual tellers and staff to specifically serve their Spanish-speaking customers. By studying banking models in other parts of the country, it was determined the best way to serve this segment was to create a separate branch to specifically serve it. Within six months, the branch opened in a strip center with clean, comfortable surroundings. Waiting rooms included sofas and chairs, as well as Spanish TV broadcasts, to accommodate entire families coming to the branch to make deposits or open an account. Customers were given computer access to enable them to communicate with family members still living in their homeland. The branch worked with the IRS to facilitate the tax identification process so accounts could be opened smoothly and conveniently. The branch also helped customers with tax preparation. To accommodate their customers' work schedules, the branch's weekday hours were extended, and Saturday and Sunday hours were added. The branch showed a profit within 90 days compared to a typical branch that usually took 18 months to break even. Three additional branches targeted to the Hispanic market have since opened, and there are plans for more. This bank proves that reaching out to serve a segment with respect, appreciation and a community spirit accounts for building good business and loyal relationships.

Targeting Profits: It always amazes me that so many companies think they must take any business that walks in the door, even if there's no profit in it. Focusing your marketing on what makes you money is pivotal. Otherwise, you are losing profits by promoting what is not making you money. How much sense does that make? Don't get caught in a loss-leader mentality. It is nonsense to think that if you get someone in the door because of a low price, they will buy more profitable products or services later on. Walmart can do this, but not small business. If your ideal market isn't the price-conscious shopper, why invite in those who are?

Targeting Efficiencies: How are you using technology to operate more efficiently and accomplish more with less? What can your technology do to free employees and you to focus on more income-generating activities? Are there procedures you can implement that make doing business with you easier than with your competition? Is there something you can do for your customers to make them more efficient with their time or resources or how they spend their money?

Universal Edge

A rubber and plastics manufacturing company was seeing steady growth by producing its product lines the same way most American manufacturers in their specialty did, through hard tooling. The father-son company, founded in 1987, focused on delivery and precision in the parts they supplied to a diverse industry base. After conducting an in-depth study of other industries and business operations, the son realized that a metal fabrication technology using software tooling could create significant efficiencies in getting his products to market. He visited the facility to see if this software tooling could be used in his company. He was so impressed, he placed an order on the spot for the $250,000 piece of equipment, which was 10 times more than his company had invested on any other single piece of equipment. The efficiencies realized were even greater than anticipated as the company could now produce in four days what used to take 30 days. In addition to producing an even higher level of accuracy, the software tooling gave them the ability to custom tool and deliver seven times faster than their competitors. The factory was also able to produce five times as many parts as they were previously. These efficiencies enabled the owners to put their strategic energies into expanding where they could leverage this technology. They began identifying industries where precision and fast turnaround were *more important than price. In only two years, the investment paid for itself. Competitors were slow in adapting, taking another seven years to make the investment. By that time, this leading-edge manufacturer had established its reputation as a company who delivered precision custom parts and could turn them around on a dime. Because they were in an ongoing mode of improvement, they were able to find ways to use the technology to meet customer needs better, faster and smarter. They had mastered the technology to the point that what used to take weeks to hard tool, they could achieve in minutes to hours with the software tooling. In one instance, an order was tooled and shipped from their dock within two hours. Forty hours later it was in the hands of the customer in Shanghai. The son takes great pride in the fact that only two hours of that 42-hour turnaround was the manufacturing process. Realizing 30 percent growth in 2010 over 2009, the company operates seven days a week with two shifts running six days a week. Now offering same-day sample turnaround and complete orders shipping within a few hours, this company understands the power and profits of targeting efficiencies as a competitive advantage.*

Targeting Morale: Are these tough times all you talk about these days? If so, get out of that gloom-and-doom mode and start focusing on what you can do to bring out positive results. Celebrate the small successes and involve everyone in your company who was a part of it. Ask your employees for ideas – you will probably be surprised by how good they are. Engage your customers and let them know why you especially appreciate them during these uncertain times. We all know our stock in relationships is priceless compared to what happens on Wall Street.

•　　•　　•

As times get more competitive, operating with a highly targeted mindset will serve your business well. A business can be diverse while it practices targeting. This is the true genius that drives growth companies. They understand that through meticulous orchestration of strategic focuses, they can set themselves apart and stay a step ahead of their competition.

20
Celebration & Recognition

If you make celebrating a year-round way of doing business, it will help turn your company into one everyone wants to be associated with. It will set you apart from your competitors. Growth companies know that these celebrations are not only good for morale, but also good for business.

Celebrate Your Relationship: Celebrate the yearly anniversary of your relationship with a client through special recognition and a token of appreciation. You can use the traditional anniversary themes as your inspiration. For example, with paper as the designated theme for year one, you could present them with an inspirational paperback book or a meaningful origami. Wikipedia has a great list if you search wedding anniversary gifts. Get creative!

Celebrate a Beginning: Many businesses celebrate a customer's birthday as a way to cement a relationship. While this is a good practice and can be meaningful, it can sometimes appear transparent, especially in a business-to-business environment. Instead, find out when customers joined their firm or began their current position. Then send a special note each year recognizing the milestone and show you pay attention.

Like Family

Talk to any client of this wealth management advisor and they will talk about him like he is the uncle, a father, or brother they always wanted in their lives. His 30-year career has seen numerous births, birthdays, weddings, college graduations, engagements and marriages on the heartwarming side. He has also seen his share of divorces, lost jobs, ailing family members and deaths on the heart wrenching side of his clients' lives. His philosophy has always been one of embracing life, even with its ups and its downs, and he made this a part of how he practiced in business. Celebrating the good times with clients through acknowledging, participating in celebrations, and being aware of special occasions was simply part of who he and his wife were as people who cared about every life they touched. He was also compassionate and strong when needed during times of strife for his clients, recognizing their anguish, disappointments, and being their confidante , serving as a practical guide to navigate their way through the storms financially and emotionally. A continuous learner and avid reader, he was always seeking opportunities to bring clients together in a positive, uplifting way to help them grow in their financial knowledge or in friendships with other clients. Events such as sponsoring a couple's cooking class with a private chef, bringing in an expert on green living, a tea luncheon and an event focused on women living their dreams, helped bring together specific clients with their journeys in mind with each thoughtful activity. His website even celebrates the unique mindsets of his three primary target markets with insight and appreciation for where each segment is in their life and work. Named among the Five Star Wealth Managers for Client Satisfaction in his market, his clients are anxious to share why he is like family with total confidence in his expertise and financial aptitude amidst the economic hazing that left many others casualties of the times.

> **Too many business owners get so caught up in their business, they forget to celebrate and recognize the big and small achievements along the way. Growth companies know how to make celebration a way of doing business internally and externally.**

Celebrate When Least Expected: Sometimes the smallest gestures can be the most memorable. One year, a raffle was occurring at a nearby church for a trip to the Bahamas for their building campaign. We decided to buy a two-dollar ticket for each client that year, and we were amazed at the response. Because it was totally unexpected, it was valued for both its uniqueness and the fact that it was for a worthy cause. None of our clients won the raffle, but some still mention it to this day. Imagine what might have happened if someone had won!

Celebrate With Purpose: Have you noticed how busy everyone seems to be? That won't change, so when planning a celebratory event, the way to get someone's attention and interest in attending is twofold. Give it a purpose and make it something out of the norm. A holiday celebration at a firm that specialized in green design made the event memorable by encouraging everyone to bring an item that they did not want, but thought someone else would want. In essence, they were encouraging people to recycle or re-gift the item. The exchange was the highlight of the party, proving that one man's junk is another man's treasure.

Celebrate Through Recognition: The news media is filled with information about people who have been promoted, achieved professional certifications or won awards. You'll be amazed by the positive vibes you create when you send a congratulatory note acknowledging accomplishments of those you do business with. While e-mails get deleted, I guarantee a card with a clipping of the announcement you read will get kept as a memento because it is so unusual. So don't hesitate to acknowledge the old-fashioned way.

•　　　•　　　•

Make your own style of celebration a part of your business inside and outside its walls. Not only does is reinforce that you take nothing for granted, it also gives others even more reason to want to be a part of the fun.

21

The WOW Factor

The sad reality is that customer service is a dying art form in America. Companies simply do not seem to care as much as they once did. One gets a return phone call and the person returning the call is deemed a standout. One is given a smile, eye contact and a welcome and it is deemed an exception versus the rule. One actually gets an answer on the first couple of rings versus voicemail and they are surprised and rendered speechless at a live person actually answering the phone.

Some blame it on the Internet and how things have gotten more impersonal over the years. Some blame it on the fact that people are in a hurry and want convenience and "cheap" over quality and attention. Some blame it on the younger generation not knowing or being taught any better, while others blame it on the older generation being tired and unhappy with having to work longer in life. The reality is none of these are right and all of these are right. The true reason customer service has gone by the wayside is plain and simple – businesses have gotten fat and lazy.

In a down economy, businesses shift from fat and lazy to lean and mean. And I mean "mean" as in crotchety. Frustrated by business not coming in so easily, and fearful of what this means to bonuses, pay raises, and on the job security, instead of stepping up their service, companies and their employees become their own worse complaint department. It is no wonder we as consumers, in business or in life, are frustrated.

The good news for any business wanting to set themselves apart from competitors is that it can be as simple as just providing good service on a very basic level. Take for instance the plumbing contractor who promised to return a call within two hours. Or perhaps the doctor's office who promised to see a patient within 15 minutes of checking in to the front desk. Consider the company who decided that someone would answer the phone in person versus a caller going straight to voicemail. In all cases, one simple act set them apart from competitors. In the case of the plumbing contractor, he set himself apart from an entire industry known for not returning calls, not showing up on time or at all, and not being considerate of the homeowner's time in general.

Growth companies take the idea of serving their customers to an entirely higher standard. They are not just focused on serving their customers. These companies are focused on "wowing" their customers. They have made it an operational priority in their business, not just a marketing focus. Consider how you can shift from a service mindset to a wowing mindset.

Sense of Pride: When a customer is proud to do business with you, they share it with others. They want people to know their needs were met and they got the products and answers they were looking for from a company that's a cut above the rest. How can you create a sense of pride in doing business with you? Have you won awards? Have you achieved something no one else in your industry has accomplished? Do you have an approach that is not only unique, but proprietary? Make sure your customers know and make them the center of why it's significant.

Sense of Purpose: When business is driven by an underlying purpose that benefits its customers, they feel engaged and a part of something meaningful. Have you defined a mission for your company that gets to the very heart of what matters most to your customers? Do you reinforce it in ways your customers can relate to and appreciate?

> *Ask anyone what the problem is with business today, and the first thing they will mention is poor customer service. Growth businesses have not lost sight of this critical success factor. They embrace customer service with even more gusto during slow economic times because they know this is when others will really screw it up.*

Signature Service

When three doctors formed a 24/7 membership-based concierge medical practice, they knew the concept would be hard for some people to believe. A doctor who is always on call? A doctor who makes house calls? Appointments the same or next day? A doctor who gives his or her cell phone number and actually answers it? The list goes on. But this is exactly what this concierge primary care practice set out to do. Initially targeting busy, high-level executives who travel at a moment's notice and need non-threatening health issues tended to when convenient, the practice has since evolved to one with a diverse patient base who wants to truly be taken care of and have a personable and open relationship with their physician. By paying an annual membership fee, members get the preferential treatment these doctors think should be standard medical procedure. In addition to being totally

accessible to patients, their offices are outfitted with labs,
x-ray rooms, and many other ancillary services so
whatever needs to be done for the patient can be done
conveniently. The waiting room is like a lobby in a fine
hotel, and examination rooms have piped-in music. All
this creates a warm, elegant ambience instead of a cold,
sterile environment. As one of the doctors explains, the
medical practice system has evolved into a protocol that
literally prevents physicians from having any quality
time with their patients. Practices have become more of a
numbers game than a healthcare provider. By examining
what was really important to a specific segment of
patients, these doctors have built a practice that is among
the top 50 fastest growing firms in its market area. Best
of all, patients from a wide range of socioeconomic
backgrounds are signing up. All this proves that you get
what you pay for and that what you pay for is actually
the best deal of all when it comes to peace of mind and
caring for one's health.

Sense of Passion: Passion is contagious. You know passion drives your business when everyone truly loves and enjoys what they are doing. Everyone benefits from it. Customers not only don't want to leave, they cannot wait to come back and be a part of the fun, energy and excitement. When your business is a place to experience rather than just a place to buy services or products, you put yourself into a whole new realm of excellence compared to your competition.

Sense of Priority: Companies that understand how to "wow" a customer are more focused on the customer being number one rather than the customer always being right. Think about this for a minute. If the customer is always right, why do they need you? If your business is a service or consulting company, they are looking to you for answers, not to simply say yes to whatever they think they need.

Sense of Power: Companies that make their customers number one also give them choices. Choices give customers a sense of empowerment that makes them feel they are in control. Have you devised package levels so a customer can choose according to budget, time or convenience? Have you articulated ways in which a customer can get more value or save more with options that cater to both?

• • •

Take a step back and consider all the ways you can serve your customers better. Look at what your competitors are not doing and make that your benchmark starting point. Pick just a handful of areas to truly excel in and show your customers how they mean everything to you. Once you are beating your competitors in customer service, strive to continually "best" yourself. When you are raising the bar in wowing yourself, you are definitely wowing your customers.

REFERRAL
RELATIONS

22

Beyond Customers

Let's get one thing clear right from the get-go. A strong referral program does not generate increased referrals from your existing customers. Building referrals should be focused less on customers and be focused more on everyone else who can create a "buzz" about your business. If you are distinguishing your capabilities and products, providing excellent customer service and delivering on promises (or better yet, delivering more than promised), your customers will gladly refer you to a multitude of others. So stay focused on wowing them with quality, service, mindfulness, consistency and enthusiasm. If you do this on an ongoing basis, the referrals will come.

You may be quite content with the referrals gained from your customers. If that is the case, I say excellent. Building a true referral marketing program may not be one of your top priorities or strategies. But if you are interested in significant growth for your business that takes only a little bit of time, consider the following statistics gained from our 2004 research.

Companies with 50 percent or more growth over a three-year period were less likely to rely solely on client referrals for growth. In addition, 95 percent of these companies received referrals from contacts other than clients, vendors or employees and their families. Another interesting finding is that 70 percent of these companies gained referrals from competitors!

Growth companies receive a continuous flow of referrals from a variety of places. Take a look at this list and see how many of these sources provide referrals for your company.

Customers	Suppliers and Vendors
Employees and Families	Civic & Charitable Affiliations
Service Providers	Business Associates
Professional Affiliations	Competitors
A Mere Acquaintance	Someone You've Never Met!

Gaining referrals from this diverse of a group requires a strong marketing outreach and an intentional strategy. Add to the list those contacts in businesses also seeking to serve the same market as you are serving, and you can start to see the powerful force you could have out in the marketplace.

To gain a better understanding of how powerful gaining referrals is to your business' bottom line, consider the following statistics I have gathered through 26 years in business that I classify as your Return on Referral. Consider where you are spending your energies after reading these comparisons.

Cold Lead: A cold lead is the equivalent of a cold call. The standard rule of thumb is that you need to make 100 calls to get one appointment. This means you have about a one percent chance that the person you connect with will become a customer. This alone should discourage you or your staff from cold calling.

Lead Referral: A lead referral is when someone mentions to you that a business or person may need your services or products. However, they don't want you to use their name because it is information they just became privy to. I equate this to a rumor. While a little better than a cold lead, it has no real legitimacy until you get more information. You have about a five percent chance of converting this kind of lead into a paying customer.

Compare a one percent chance a cold lead will become a customer to a 95 percent chance that someone who's received your company's name from multiple referrals will become one, and you can easily figure out where your company's time is better spent.

Identified Referral: In this instance, the individual giving you the referral allows you to use their name and to share the fact they referred you. This offers more credibility and increases your chances of converting the prospect to a customer to about 15 percent. It can increase to 25 percent if you are given more detailed information to be better prepared when making the contact.

Contacted Referral: This scenario is getting more ideal. The person referring you not only shares the opportunity with you, but personally calls or e-mails the prospect to introduce you and to share the reasons you are being referred. It increases the likelihood this kind of prospect will become a customer to between 35 and 45 percent. This is getting closer to what you ultimately want in a referring relationship.

Multiple Referrals: In all of the above scenarios, it was up to you to initiate contact with the prospect once a referral was generated. But when someone receives multiple referrals to one company after asking several people for recommendations, you are placed in the enviable position where the prospect comes to you. Best of all, this increases the likelihood they will become a customer to 95 percent. When someone is getting strong recommendations from several unbiased sources, you have created a virtual sales force that has you top of mind 24/7.

Quality of Contacts: One of the most important things to remember about your referral network is that it is not so much about quantity of contacts as it is about their quality. You should not only expect referrals, but also give them for those who are referring you. If you are not confident enough in their abilities to refer them, they should not be part of your referral network. You must be willing to reciprocate.

Caring Connections

In 2000, the husband-wife owners of a franchise that provided non-medical in-home care services entered the marketplace ahead of the curve. This enabled them to build solid connections and a strong reputation before competitors began moving into the area. Because they had a national operational and marketing support network and were the first full-service provider in the area, they experienced significant growth for several years in a row. As competition entered the market, they continued their double-digit growth because they knew what was critical to their business: relationships. One key to their success was the personal approach they took in building long-term and mutually beneficial connections. They set out to be a valued resource and support for all healthcare professionals and organizations serving the community's senior citizens. They considered it their personal mission to be advocates for seniors and their families. When issues arose, they leveraged the knowledge of experts from across the country for answers and then shared them with professionals or client families. Both owners maintained high-profile involvement on a variety of boards, committees and councils devoted to senior issues. They offered their firm's time, talent and resources to The Alzheimer's Association, hospitals and health fair events. They created a Professional Unwind event for social workers that is now held three times a year and attracts about 200 people. They embraced the national "Be a Santa to a Senior" program, providing more than 1,100 seniors in their market area with needed items over the holidays in 2009. Growing from 100 employees in 2002 to more than 200 in 2010, the company has built one of the top in-home non-medical care franchises in the U.S. It generates 80 percent of its business through referrals from its many valued connections in the community and is a model for franchises across the country to emulate.

Mere Acquaintances: If you are getting referrals from casual acquaintances, you know you have a solid referral marketing program in place. Strategic involvement in key professional, industry or business organizations will foster referrals from acquaintances. Chances are that even though you have only briefly met these individuals, they have been paying close attention to you from afar and are impressed by your business and how you approach your commitments.

People You've Never Met: Ongoing public relations that generate regular announcements about the business, combined with a strong Internet presence, is how many companies get referrals from people they have never met. Someone reads an article and then shares with someone seeking your services or products. Someone notices your branded vehicles on the road and mentions your company to a neighbor or co-worker looking for what you have to offer.

• • •

You should be communicating with your referral network on a regular basis, keeping them informed of what you are doing, just as you do with your customers. Done strategically, referral marketing that goes beyond your customer base will reap tremendous benefits for your company's growth. So take a look at how you can incorporate a referral marketing program into your strategy. Your time is well spent engaging others to promote your company.

23
Coopetition

How you view your competition could be why your business is struggling while others are not. Why? Because if you view them as the enemy, you are most likely missing opportunities to grow your business in ways you have never anticipated. There is another way to view your competition from a collaborative perspective. I call this coopetition.

Direct vs. Indirect: I am continuously amazed by the number of business owners who are unclear about the difference between direct and indirect competitors – or claim they have no competition. If you believe you have no competition, why aren't you lounging on the beach and enjoying the money flowing in without even lifting a finger? Sarcasm aside, the real opportunity in knowing your competition – even those who are not direct competitors – is the ways in which you can potentially help one another and leverage each others' strengths instead of only focusing on weaknesses.

A direct competitor is a business that pursues the same target market as you, offers a comparable scope of services and products, and operates within the same market space. An indirect competitor can be classified in a variety of ways. Some are companies that offer the same services and products, but target a different customer base. Some target the same customers as you, but only offer a portion of the services or products.

There is a saying that goes: "Keep your friends close and your enemies closer." While this is said in a spirit of mistrust, the real opportunity is identifying those direct and indirect competitors with whom you share a great deal of mutual respect. With the view that good companies get business and there is plenty to share, competitors can ingeniously grow together while others go out of business.

United in Caring

The founder of an acupuncture, herbal medicine and therapeutic massage practice knew from his years as a massage therapist that the biggest mistake made by many in the alternative medicine industry was positioning themselves as a replacement for typical medical care.

This astute practitioner had developed solid relationships based on mutual respect with professionals in both the medical and alternative medicine sides of healthcare. The common factor among all of them was a commitment to doing what would best serve patients for their long-term good health and wellbeing. As a result, from the first day of his practice he sought to collaborate and work as a cooperative member of an overall healthcare advisory and provider team. His spirit of unification served him well as therapists, chiropractors and medical doctors referred patients to him. They knew they would be kept informed and their role respected in the care of their mutual patients. He also took a proactive role in educating the marketplace that further enhanced his reputation within the lake community where he practices. By understanding the real value of cooperation, not only are patients gaining the best healthcare in the area, but this professional and his colleagues are seeing growth in all of their practices.

Operational Capacity & Overflow: Indirect competitors are of great value in both slow and boom economic times. During slow times that may require you to make operational cuts, you can outsource to them the services you have eliminated. During boom times, these indirect competitors can notch up your capacity by covering overflow when your company is at capacity.

> *Our research found that during the economic downturn after 9-11, 75 percent of high-growth companies received referrals from and gave referrals to competitors. More than 50 percent formed strategic alliances with competitors to pursue joint opportunities.*

Sharing Customers: In Secret #5, you learned about profit sizing your products and services to identify the ones that are the most and least profitable. Growth companies understand how important this is to their bottom line and in determining where to focus their marketing attention. In addition, they understand the power of friendly competition whose profit centers are different and complementary. When times get tough, instead of spending valuable resources on less profitable work, these savvy businesses form strategic relationships to share customers with each focusing on their most profitable areas. While other competitors run themselves out of business taking any work – including that which costs them money – these collaborative competitors grow both profits and sales.

Reassigning Customers: In Secret #19, you learned about segmenting and targeting within your business as a means of being more strategically focused in serving your customers. This is another way growth companies use relationships with competitors to effectively serve customers while also making shifts where needed. Smart growth-minded companies transition customers who are no longer a good target or profit center to competitors still focusing on the sector. To these companies, it is more important to be viewed as having customers' best interests in mind even if it is in their best interest to do business with someone else.

•   •   •

Another reason to look at indirect competitors is that they may be a potential acquisition. Many companies get broadsided by not paying attention to indirect competitors only to find them merge and become a force to be reckoned with as a new direct competitor. Keeping a finger on the pulse on your competition should be first and foremost about leveraging the information to your customers' and your advantage. If this means cooperating with a competitor in order to better serve your customer, you have just proven how important your customers truly are to your business.

24

Cross Promotion

As a business owner you are never in business alone, and this especially holds true when it comes to marketing your business. Too many businesses are not using all of their available resources and options wisely to cost effectively get their business in front of qualified buyers. One often overlooked opportunity is in cross promotion with other businesses going after the same markets as your business.

Part of the reason this is overlooked is because companies have not done a good job of profiling their ideal customer (Secret #13), so they have not identified those businesses seeking the same exact profile. Another reason this is overlooked is because they are hesitant to share their customer list with others out of concern it will be viewed as a breech of privacy. In some cases, this would be true and should be guarded depending on the business you are in. However, in most cases, when a customer's needs and desires are closely understood, the opportunity to know of another business that could serve them in the same way with a complimentary service or product is appealing and appreciated.

After you have identified businesses that are going after the same exact profile of customer, then you need to narrow your list down to those who also share the same values and philosophies in how they operate their businesses. This is because if they share the same values and philosophies, then they are also attracting and serving your ideal psychographic profile too, which we now know is extremely important to appealing to your most qualified prospects. Another reason this is important is because you want to take pride in the businesses which you are associated and not fall into a "guilt by association" scenario.

Sharing Insights & Perspective: Since it is likely some of your existing customers patronize a potential cross promotional partner, put a communication out to your customers to see if some of them have done business with the business. If you get good reviews, then proceed to approach. If no one has experienced the potential promotional partner because it is new to the area, then seek perspective as to what would be appealing to your customer base as feedback you can share with the prospective partner. This will be appreciated and also open the door to discussion because you have gained valuable input from either their existing customers or potential customers of yours who could be future customers for them.

Sharing Promotional Investment: Notice I have entitled this an investment – not an expense. As explained in Secret #9, too many businesses categorize marketing efforts as an expense. Chances are, some of your potential cross promotional partners view marketing as an expense. This can work to your advantage when you approach them about sharing the costs of a joint promotion. For example, by splitting the investment to prepare a direct mail campaign that is sent to your combined lists, both of you can stretch your dollars. Creating a destination event with nearby businesses can be a highly effective means of cross promotion. Tie it into an arts organization to display works of art and feature local acoustical musicians and you have created an "art crawl" event that is replicable and supports the community.

Co-packaging Offerings: Another opportunity is to expand your cross promotional effort beyond awareness and joint promotion to combine your products or services. Businesses serving other businesses may offer a promotional partner's product in conjunction with a service they are promoting. You could also join together to present an educational program or a lunch-and-learn program, either on location or via a webinar or teleseminar. On the consumer side, businesses can package their products and services at a special price exclusive to customers of the participating businesses. A realtor established strong relationships with several businesses, including a maid service, lawn maintenance company, spa,

> *Nine out of ten high-growth companies understood their customer base so well that they also knew the types of other businesses, services or professionals customers valued and used on a regular basis. More than 60 percent leveraged cross promotion opportunities on a regular basis.*

veterinary clinic, physician practice and home accessories retailer. By carefully selecting businesses a new homeowner would patronize, the realtor was viewed as a godsend to her clients who were handed special introductory pricing and an immediate array of service providers and retailers they would patronize. The possibilities are only limited by the imagination and creativity of you and your cross promotional partner. However, be sure that whatever you do makes sense and appeals to your mutual customer databases.

Not Another Fish Tale

You'd think that when the economy took a nosedive, a fishing excursion business located in a lake community would sink right along with it. However, a savvy captain with an entrepreneurial mindset simply saw the downturn as a welcomed challenge. It was no different than catching an elusive bass on the lake or a great white on the open sea. He had already established a strong brand for his business through a fishing column that ran in several local papers. He was active in a number of local organizations, so he was well-known in the community. When the downturn began in 2008, corporate excursions disappeared as companies cut spending. Local residents also cut back on their leisure activities. The captain put his marketing cap on to ride the wave with calculated strategies that paid off in a record year of business in 2009. First, he understood he was in business to create a fun experience for his customers. So he stepped beyond the fishing realm and offered sunset cruises, lake excursions and packages for those opting for "staycations" to save money. He sought out businesses going after the same market profile so that they could leverage their promotional power together for special exclusive offerings. For example, a day at a spa was combined with a sunset cruise on the lake. He formed cross promotional relationships with businesses such as a yacht retailer, hotels and a log home manufacturer. His marketing genius reached another level when he decided to offer gift certificates for the holidays. His belief that residents would embrace giving a loved one the gift of fun on the lake paid off. November and December are typically his slowest sales months, yet he realized a 300 percent increase in December. His 2009 sales beat 2008 sales by 32 percent. Ask this entrepreneurial captain if it is a good day to go fishing, and he will reply, "Every day is a good day when you make it a fun day."

Sharing Customer Lists: One of the simplest and best ways to ease into a cross promotional relationship is by sharing your customer lists. However, make sure each of your customer bases is aware you are sharing the list. Or protect your lists by having each of you send any special promotion materials about the other business to your own database. As customers begin to patronize the other business, it can confirm the contact information and gain permission to add these new customers to its database. If privacy is important to both your customer bases, this is a clever way to cross promote while being protective and respectful of your customers' wishes. Another way to share each other's lists is to use them for research to gain insight about current and future offerings. Each business alerts a sampling of its customers that the other business is going to be contacting them. A special token of appreciation can be offered by both businesses as a way of expressing thanks to the customer for completing a survey or being interviewed. Another way to leverage one another's lists is to conduct a combined focus group asking for customer feedback on new products and planned joint promotions.

•　　•　　•

The opportunity to gain insight and access to a pre-qualified captive ideal market can produce a significant return on investment when done strategically in a win-win spirit of cooperation. Begin to compile your list of possible cross promotional partners today. Your customers will thank you for helping them find other providers as wonderful as you, and your partners will appreciate the opportunity to use all your combined resources more effectively.

25

Circles of Influence

You know you have created a powerful referral network when you are literally in the right place *all* the time. This means you don't have to be physically present to be in the minds of people who refer business to you. You are the first business to come to mind because you have achieved a penetration level in your market that is envied by your competitors and valued by those who refer you because you make them look good.

The ability to garner multiple referrals is exponentially increased when you understand all the ways you can expand your circles of influence. When your company is being recommended by a variety of contacts from throughout the community and your industry, you have achieved an awareness level that will ensure business comes in even when the economy slows. When times are tough, people gravitate to those who have earned the most confidence from others.

Employees & Family: The greatest advocates for high-growth companies are their employees and their families. You only need to sit around a dinner table or watch a children's soccer game to know that conversations inevitably turn to work. People who are delighted and eager to share how wonderful it is to work for your company are telling people it's also a good place to do business.

Vendors & Suppliers: How you treat your vendors and suppliers will also become known in the marketplace. While your suppliers and vendors may also serve your competitors, they still have their favorites. They will respond with referrals like any other contact who values what you bring to the market. If you are concerned that if you share your plans with vendors and suppliers, it will get out to your competitors, you are operating from a scarcity mindset rather than a growth mindset.

Yes Man

An audio video installation sales manager determined he could go it on his own, and so established his company in the fall of 2007. With thirteen years of relationships to back him up, he and a partner quickly had five projects

on the docket and more streaming in. As the economy
began to move south, competitors began to close their
doors, but not this company. Its owner believed that a
positive mental attitude was everything and maintaining
quality relationships would continue to serve him and
his business well. He was right. Since the inception of
his business he determined he would be a self-appointed
ambassador within the various circles of influence he
was involved in. In spite of the economy's downturn, he
continued to focus on how he could help his vendors be a
success right along with him. While others cut back their
community or industry involvements due to "needing to
focus on their business," he
considered his involvements a
critical part of what had and
would continue to make his
business a success. When others
spoke about the tough times, he
would shift the focus to the
opportunities. He believed that
if you focus on negative aspects,
you view the world that way. He
enjoyed helping others see what
could be, not just what was, and
he became known as a person to
connect with for a lead, a
supplier or any kind of resource.
While other AV companies went
out of business, this company
realized a 30 percent increase in
profits in 2009 over 2008 with
the level expected to double in 2010. It just goes to show,
that when you say, "Yes I can!" you can!

> **High-growth companies realize that anyone they interact with has the potential to send a positive or negative vibe about what it is like to do business with them. They understand the "talk factor" is the most powerful image builder or business destructor if not respected for the power it possesses.**

There are many other ways to build positive connections to expand your circle of referral influence. In addition to those you conduct business with or interact with on a regular basis, networking, and referral groups are also good options to consider.

Networking Meetings: A variety of groups have been formed with the sole purpose of helping businesses make connections. The problem with many of these groups is that they offer a means of meeting and greeting, but there is no real meat behind the process to give attendees a true understanding of each other's services or products. Nor is there an opportunity for gaining an understanding of a business contact's ideal target customers. In many cases, the event is a large gathering that is more social than informational. While enjoyable, it may not be the best use of your or your employees' time. Try to find out the agenda and main purpose and how the group helps businesses connect. Ones that offer industry exclusivity at least give you the opportunity to be the only one in the group doing what you do. However, if there is no formal approach or ability to directly present your business and its offerings on a captive level, you are spending your time on superficial efforts rather than substantive ones.

Referral vs. Leads Groups: Taking networking meetings to another level, leads or referral groups concentrate on a more intimate group of businesses (about 20-40) with industry exclusivity. Seek out groups that focus on referrals rather than leads. A referral group is genuinely interested in bringing more business to all the participants and in facilitating their doing business together. A leads group provides the names of people members have come in contact with since the last meeting. The names are placed in the jar for whoever wants to pursue them. Typically conducted over a meal, the ideal group gives members opportunities to share news, talk about business and learn about each other's companies. Your ideal group should have several members going after the same market as you. If at least half of the members do not, look for a group with the right mix of businesses for you.

●　　●　　●

In Secrets #31 through #37, you will learn even more about how to increase your circles of influence beyond what was discussed in this secret. Knowledge is power, but so is who you know and how you continually prove you are worthy of their trust and confidence.

INTERNET
PRESENCE

26

Virtual Receptionist

Your website is your business's most powerful 24/7 promotional tool. If you don't have a website, many people will never know you exist. Just because you are not conducting actual transactions over the Internet doesn't mean you are not selling through your website. It attracts customers to your business and is a portal for those who comparison-shop.

In the mid-1990s, a company with a locally-focused customer base could get away with not having a website. Just a few years later, it was obvious an Internet presence was becoming the wave of the future in how business was being conducted. A business with a Web presence was steps ahead of its competition in significant ways.

Consumer businesses were the first to understand the power of this new medium. Business-to-business firms and companies providing services are still catching up. Hopefully, this section will convince those of you without an Internet presence that a website is absolutely essential to your business operations and promotion.

Virtual Credibility: Having a website is the primary means by which people find a business. You are expected to have one. A business is not viewed as being credible or well established if it does not have a website. If you don't have a website, you're going to lose customers to companies who do – even if you serve just a small market with a 10-mile radius. Those who are aware of your business will be surprised you don't have a website. They will perceive you as not staying up with your buying public.

Virtual Introduction: Your website is the portal many will use to explore your business and determine its merit for their hard-earned dollars. The secret to its effectiveness lies in what you communicate on your homepage. This creates a first impression for your business. It introduces your business and should immediately distinguish it from competitors in an inviting, compelling way. Your homepage is the key to successfully nurturing early-stage buyers by getting them to come back or explore your site further. Site navigation – particularly its ease of use and accessibility – is another important factor to consider when designing your website. Can visitors on the site get to where they want to go in only a few clicks?

Click Friendly

An Internet solutions provider understood all too well the impact that a website's homepage and ease of navigation have in creating a powerful marketing tool for a business. When creating its own website, the ownership team, designers and programmers were determined to demonstrate how a website can be a virtual receptionist to prospects and clients. They included all the information a prospect needed to make a decision to engage the company. They considered all the most frequently asked questions received by tech support. They developed a site map and navigation system that enabled both prospects and clients to get where they needed to go in a few easy clicks. For prospects, this included package options, work portfolios, in-depth service listings and pages where they could sign up for the company newsletter or request information via e-mail. For clients, the site provided online access to training references for the company's two managed content platforms, support guides and instructions for e-mail access, file transfer and server information and instructions on how to create a password-protected site and numerous other support initiatives, all to assist clients find solutions before they had to call tech support. The company's growth has proven it practices what it preaches. For several years, it has been ranked number one in its marketplace for providing easy-to-maintain websites and Internet solutions for clients.

In our studies with thousands of customers of clients over ten years, companies that had websites were more likely to get better qualified referral inquiries. Why? Because the website was the first place their customers would tell those they referred to go.

Some basic information to consider posting to your site include:

- Directions to location(s)
- Hours of operation
- Departments or divisions
- Physical address
- Phone and fax numbers
- Contact emails

You also need to understand why existing customers visit your site. This is critical to making it an efficient receptionist and assistant for your business during off-hours. Areas to consider including on your site are:

- Frequently asked questions
- Regularly requested documents
- Troubleshooting guides
- Quick help tips
- Resource links
- Reference listings

You only need to consider what customers most commonly ask about when they call you. This will guide you in determining what will be of value on your website.

Virtual Qualifier: Today's consumers are well-educated, and the Internet is their chief tool for gathering information about purchases. So use your website as a way to help visitors qualify themselves as an ideal match for your business. As stated earlier in Secret #13, the main goal of marketing is to attract those you want as customers and to discourage those you do not. Your website is the perfect place to start. Consider how your website effectively addresses these key decision-making factors:

- Who You Serve: Does your website clearly and effectively segment and target those you serve most effectively? Will your ideal market want to do business with your company because of what they read and see on your site? Are they able to go right to a page that speaks directly to them – and then feel you really know who they are and how they think? The more your site visually and verbally speaks to your ideal target markets, the more likely you are to convert them from visitors to buyers. Consider having a "Who We Serve" section that addresses this issue.

- Values: Something pivotal happened after the tragedy of 9-11. Our values and what we hold most dear changed and were elevated, not only in our everyday lives, but in everything we did from that day on. People have made shared values a criteria for who they choose to associate and do business with. When you share your company values – often deep-seated ones based on your own personal values – you give your company personality and character. It tells your ideal market you know what is important to them because it is important to you, too.

- <u>Benefits vs. Features</u>: Consumers compare features, benefits and price comparisons when making buying decisions. Benefits should clearly differentiate why your products or services are a better choice based on what customers want. Many companies confuse benefits with features. They wonder why prospects don't understand how they differ from the competition and are preferable. When customers understand the benefits gained from their purchase, price becomes less important, especially if added value is perceived. To help you better understand this concept, here is a comparison of features and benefits.

Features	Benefits
How it looks	What it does better
How it operates	Problem solved
What is included	Value added results
Steps or process	What is achieved

- <u>Direct Comparisons</u>: Once online buyers do their comparisons, they typically narrow their choices to one to three possible suppliers. One of the best pages you can have on your site is one that compares your products or way of approaching business with others. It does not have to be a direct comparison calling attention to a specific competitor. It can be as simple as Our Way vs. Their Way, Our Approach vs. Traditional Approach, or Our Program vs. Their System. Then succinctly list comparisons, giving those visiting your site an arsenal of information to consider when visiting competing sites. Since most other sites will not have this level of insight, yours will stand out.

- <u>Ease in Inquiring</u>: A majority of online searchers prefer to complete an online form rather than call a business because they often use the Internet during off-hours when businesses are closed. They also often prefer to avoid talking to a salesperson until they have a clearer idea of what they are looking for. Gain a clear understanding of the typical information your target market needs to know and how you can better serve prospective customers. Ask for this information in your easy-to-complete online form. Always include a section that allows visitors to add additional comments. When you receive the form, your sales team will be able to follow-up with specific information. This will help close the deal faster and easier.

●   ●   ●

Once you realize your website is the first impression Internet users get of your business, you will become empowered to leverage its immense communication power to reach your target market. When you realize it can also be a means of serving your customers during off-hours, you will become even more valuable to them. They will know you are a business that understands what it truly means to be accessible.

27
Virtual Tool

Growth companies use the Internet daily to access information, identify resources, find support, and promote and operate their businesses. They understand that technology is a critical means to success. You should be leveraging the technology of the Internet in a multitude of ways to make your company more successful. Your website should be more than a virtual receptionist – it needs to evolve into a true marketing and operational tool that attracts your ideal customers.

Resource Center: If you want to be a one-stop resource and a total-solutions provider for your customer base, make this aspect of your website stand out. Provide information based on what your target market wants to utilize on a regular basis.

Click & Presto

A 30-year-old commercial printing company has been able to stand out in its market by understanding the power of service. It understood that staying ahead of customer needs would give it a competitive advantage. It embraced each growth opportunity with foresight and a focus on being a resource to its customers. When the digital revolution occurred, it was ready. When environmentally-friendly printing practices entered the marketplace, it set the standard by being first. It became one the first in its region to offer certified Forestry Stewardship Council printing. Always seeking ways to differentiate itself and be a resource to its clients, the company brought the same level of commitment to its website. While other printing companies offered the ability to place orders securely on an FTP site, this company's customers were given an entire arsenal of resources and support in a special tab entitled My Order

Desk. Available resources included tips and tricks, links for all supported software programs and standard file creation issues, an A-Z glossary of terms, links to resources of interest, and an exhaustive publications list. A support center featured a knowledge-based search to allow visitors to get instant answers to common questions, with no busy signals or telephone tag. A login account section allowed clients to submit a project for an estimate, place an order or reorder and track its status. Despite all these conveniences, the site was viewed as a way to enhance customer service, not as a way to replace good old-fashioned personal service. When customers called or placed an order, the human touch remained a high priority from concept to delivery. While many commercial printing operations have been forced to make cutbacks, this company continues to add employees and equipment to meet the demands of its expanding client base. It proves each and every day that high tech combined with high touch is a surefire way to run a high-growth business.

> **In the CRISP Principle study, high-growth companies use the Internet daily for information, resources and support of their operations and their marketing. The Internet is a tool that helps these businesses run better and lets their customers and prospects know them better.**

Articles & Reports: If you are positioning your company as a go-to expert, grow your website by using it to share your expertise with articles, newsletters and reports on a regular basis. To build an even larger following, encourage visitors to sign up to automatically receive these updates, which should include links to your website.

News & Developments: Include news items about your business in a News and Events page of your website. A simple way to start is to include a Latest Developments page that succinctly recaps news in a couple of sentences in a chronological order, with the most recent posting first. If you send news releases to the media, post them on your website in real time. News about any events your company is hosting or participating in should also be posted.

Virtual Tours & Demos: Streaming video is becoming more affordable and also easier for people to view and download. So consider adding video clips to your website. These can include tours of your facility or product demonstrations. Think about other ways you can use video to introduce your business or reinforce what you do in your market.

Webinars & Telewebinars: Webinars and telewebinars are the fastest-growing means of online interactive learning. Webinars often do not require an actual live presentation and can be posted and accessed at viewers' convenience. But they can also be scheduled events set for a particular time that people login to watch. Telewebinars combine web-based training with telephone communications to allow live instruction via the Internet. This enables participants to chat or enter questions for feedback from the instructor via a moderator. GoToMeetings offers a platform for setting up and moderating webinars and telewebinars.

Webcasts & Podcasts: Businesses are realizing the power of broadcasting information through their website visually or audibly. Webcasts through a Skype account or webcam offer the ability to make key announcements at a scheduled time and then download them to your site for viewing afterwards. MP3 players and other electronic listening devices are used for more than just listening to a playlist of music. If you know the decision-makers in your ideal target market are always on the go, make it easy for them to get information from you with downloadable podcasts.

Surveys & Polls: Offering links to surveys can be an interactive way to engage visitors and capture information you can use in your business. Invite your customers to participate and make it easy for them to reach these tools from your homepage. In the case of a survey, change the questions as situations develop in your industry or the marketplace. Once enough data has been obtained, you can share the results with the participants, as well as to your database as a whole for added traction.

Self Assessment & Discovery Tools: One way to make people choose your company over the competition is to give prospective customers the ability to do an initial self assessment related to your offerings. An assessment or short quiz that helps individuals gain insights about themselves or their business can motivate them to inquire about how you can help them. This unobtrusive means of visitors self-assessing their areas of concern can help set you apart.

• • •

As you can see, there are numerous ways to transform your website from an introduction to a destination on the Internet. One part of the magic is how you pack the site with useful, easily accessible information for your target market. The other part is how you continually remind them and invite them in.

28

Dynamic vs. Stagnant

Gone are the days when a website serves only as an online brochure. Internet users expect and deserve more. This not only applies to individuals who surf the Internet, but also to the search engines that direct users to websites. Search engines include sights such as Google, Yahoo, Bing and Ask.com. If you think your website was finished when it went live, you are missing the mark. A website is a growing entity just like your business. If you want people to view your business as a dynamic entity, your website should reflect the same attitude and evolve with your business. You didn't start your business only to let it stagnate. So you should not create a website without plans to keep adding to it. Make it a reflection of how your business continues to evolve and grow.

Building a website that can continually grow requires planning. In Secrets #26 and #27, you learned about a website's various components that can help it achieve more for your business. But before you put these components together, prioritize what will be most appealing to your target market for the greatest impact. Doing this will help avoid the need to rebuild your site over and over again.

Understanding the pros and cons of different website-building approaches is important. Too many websites are built with platforms that can't be expanded, do not interact well with search engines or are difficult to use. No matter how cool you think your website is, it is not effective unless it produces leads, inquiries, and ultimately sales

Download & Go: When building your website, do not confuse dynamic with dramatic special effects. Flash introductions and funky music welcoming visitors to your site has proven to be more of a deterrent than an attraction. Why? Ninety-three percent of individuals admit they access their computer at work for personal reasons. When they decide to take a five-minute break to conduct some of that personal business, the last thing they want is for everyone in the company to know they are on a non-business-related website. Skip the fancy fanfare and allow your graphics to reinforce your brand. Allow your visitors to get right to the website without any delays or distractions. Otherwise, your potential customers may be clicking away as fast as they clicked on the initial link that found you.

Quick-Study Access: Visitors may find your site through a search engine, but once they get there, they don't want to have to search any more. People are generally impatient to begin with, and technology has made them even more impatient. When it comes to the Internet, we want what we want immediately. If it takes longer than we think it should, we move on – plain and simple. We want to get to the information we are seeking right away and not have to do a lot of thinking to get there. Regardless of what industry you are in, consider how your market wants to navigate your website and build it to accommodate those preferences.

Access Success

A donated-goods reseller and workforce development services organization did not want its website to be just another company website listing information like an encyclopedia. Their goal was to create a more user-friendly experience to give people a reason to come back and spend time on the site. To accomplish this, the website includes interactive areas for each of the services offered by the organization. For their workforce development services, the website includes embedded video success stories from program graduates, online and downloadable training applications and class schedules, in-depth information about the programs and services offered and a career FAQ section. To insure that the agency continuously improves as the economy and workforce expectations change, there are also client, business, and referral surveys posted to the site. The down economy greatly increased the need for job training and employment services. However, it also has the potential for decreased donations and charitable giving. As a not-for-profit corporation, donations were critical to the organization, as proceeds from the sale of those items

> **If you believe building a website is just a matter of putting a visual brochure on the Web, then you are stuck in two-dimensional thinking. Your website is a virtual powerhouse of interaction and attraction when you make it a truly dynamic representation of your business.**

would fund the programs and services for those out of work. The website needed to appeal to those who would contribute as well as those looking for services. For shoppers and donors, there is an interactive zip code locator to help find the nearest store or donation center. The How-to portion of the website provides instructions for every type of donation from clothing and household goods to furniture, computers and cars, as well as tax information for donors. On the retail side, the website boasts shopping tips, the "treasure hunt" experience told by real shoppers in audio files, store locations, and standard price lists. With the Internet being a key source of information, education and customer service, the marketing team knew that its Internet presence also needed to be where shoppers, donors and potential clients connected with the organization and others. Therefore, links from and to the site connect visitors to pages on Twitter, Facebook and Flickr as well as video files on YouTube and to the agency's blog "WOW Goodwill." This virtually-driven entity realized a 300 percent increase in individuals being served in a two-year period. In 2007 within the organization's service area, there were 6,500 individuals using their services. In 2009, there were nearly 18,000 individuals served. In addition, their donations increased during a down economy in 2009 with more than 897,000 items donated redirecting 55 million pounds of waste from landfills.

Continuous Updates: Having information that requires regular updating on your website is a smart move. It makes your site a dynamic one preferred by search engines. Websites updated on a regular basis are viewed as more active. Review Secret #27 for numerous ideas on what components you can build into your website that you can update frequently.

In-house Administration: Make sure your website is programmed so you have control over basic text, photo uploads and updating. This control increases the likelihood that refreshing your website content will be an ongoing business activity for your company. I cannot emphasize this enough. When you rely on an outside contractor, it is easy for these activities to be put off or delayed. Most websites can be built so anyone can maintain them without needing special knowledge. Make this a part of the requirements for any web designer you consider hiring. No one should have a website where the access, control and ability to update content is in a third party's hands.

Reasons to Link Back In: When you post new information on your site – be it an article, a news release, an event announcement, a report, a quiz or any other new resource – it is a perfect time to send a brief e-mail to your database about it with a hyperlink to the full text on your website. Too many businesses miss the opportunity to reconnect with customers and qualified prospects to get them to return to their site. Even if the recipients do not click on the link when it is first received, they may bookmark it and go back to it at a more convenient time. This is one of the beauties of the Internet. Everyone – including your customers – has complete access 24/7.

•　　•　　•

After your website goes live, you have to work to keep it alive by adding new and valuable information to it. Make your website one your customers return to again and again and also recommend to others.

29

Beyond the Site

The Internet has made business today a "virtual" phenomenon, no longer limited by bricks and mortars, proximity or borders. Businesses that have seen the light and moved into the virtual world beyond their website have realized the true power of the Internet in ways they could not have imagined just a few years ago. Businesses that once were local or regional in market reach are now conducting business globally. First you need to understand the trends. Then you need to know how to best leverage them within your business.

Up, Up and Online: A cup of coffee and the Internet are the way modern life comes awake in the morning. Studies indicate that most people start their day about 7 a.m. with a caffeine jolt as they log on to the Internet to get their day started. People typically access the Internet first thing to catch up on e-mail, connect briefly with social media, check out the weather and surf the news before heading to work. The Internet is used more than any other media in the early morning because people can get right to the information they need rather than having to wait until it comes up on the TV or radio.

Up for Socializing & Connecting: The impact of social media on Internet usage has been phenomenal. Social media sites are the fastest growing category on the Internet, doubling in size in 2009. Facebook, Twitter and LinkedIn are the most popular and effective sites used by businesses, especially small ones. The real secret for busy small business owners is to use these sites solely for business purposes and to set them up to feed into one another. This makes them more manageable. A savvy way to get on board with social networking is to use a college intern to help you get started. If you can't pay the intern, work with a college so they can get academic credit for the experience.

Up for Entertainment & Education: Viewing videos on YouTube and downloading music on iTunes started as forms of personal entertainment. But YouTube is now a source to view business demos, news clips presentations and announcements, while people turn to iTunes to listen to business podcasts or workshops downloaded to an MP3 player. By linking websites, e-mail communications and social media, small business owners can realize the true power of bringing audio and video messages about their business to the Internet.

Up-to-the-Minute Blog & News Posts: Company blogs are becoming a common link and navigational tab on small business websites as blog postings are gaining higher rankings on search engines. By offering opinions, information, news and articles on a daily or weekly basis, many businesses are making blogging a team activity rather than putting all the responsibility on one person. Posting news releases on free newswires such as prlog.com or i-newswire.com demonstrates the power of the Internet with exposure on Google in less than an hour.

Up for Sharing & Gathering: LinkedIn and MeetUp are seeing phenomenal success in connecting like-minded business professionals in special interest groups to share information, resources, articles, insights and more with a click of the mouse. Facebook groups and event posts bring people to physical events at a business site that would have never been reached any other way. The ability to continue to share posts creates a momentum that accounts for 70 percent of the value of social media today.

> *The World Wide Web can feel like the wild west until you lasso its power beyond your website. Once you do, your business will explode with a multitude of qualified customers and opportunities, all brought to you by a common interest and the click of the mouse.*

World Wide Wow

An Internet-based nanny referral service knew that to truly be a resource, it needed to be everywhere its key target audiences communicated. To effectively set this strategy in motion, the company's website was developed as a resource and information tool so there were value-added reasons for visiting the website for families seeking a nanny as well as nannies seeking a family. Live chat capabilities offered ways for clients and prospects to get answers quickly. An expansive library of articles, books for purchase, affiliate and resource sections, video clips and more were available on the site 24/7 with a single click or two. Online optimization was an investment from the beginning, capturing visitors through targeted searches using pay-

per-click services. However, the owner knew that the key to creating massive viral awareness and interest was through connecting virtually in a multitude of ways. From LinkedIn, TwitterMoms, Facebook, and podcasts to a company blog with countless postings across the web, the company's reputation spread exactly as planned — including being utilized by TV show host, Dr. Phil, as a nanny expert on an ongoing basis. The company has branched out into babysitting and senior care referral services, as well as into Canada since its founding in 2003. Its triple-digit growth put it among the Inc. 500 for 2009.

The businesses I have worked with started out slowly, adding social media platforms with a profile on either LinkedIn or Facebook and focusing on building one network before adding another. For example, Twitter was often added with a mobile phone ability so a tweet could be texted. Tweets were then programmed to automatically be fed as posts into a Facebook or Fan page. Business owners who were also positioning themselves as experts created a personal Facebook page with posts providing thought-provoking or insightful information relevant to their expertise. The actual business and particular products would then get a Fan page.

•   •   •

The idea of adding an online presence and network beyond your website can seem overwhelming if you don't know where to begin. For this secret, I encourage you to begin slowly and then grow as you get comfortable with each online option.

30
Optimization

The Google Factor has been a way of life and a way of business for several years. Yet small businesses across America are still pouring billions of dollars into print phone book listings and phone book display advertisements. After all, it's what companies have been doing for the last 50 years – in spite of diminishing returns as people now reach for their computer mouse instead of a phone book when looking for a supplier or service provider. More than 1.5 billion people worldwide access the Internet. North America leads the globe as a result of more than 75 percent of the American population using the Internet. That's followed by Australia (60 percent) and Europe (53 percent). This confirms that the Internet is the first stop (and many times the only one) for people looking for information about a possible purchase – as well as for simply finding a phone number. It's known as the Google Factor.

The Neighborhood Myth: In 2004, 65 percent of consumers in a study of 5,000 Internet users determined their product purchases through online research. A quarter of these users specifically researched products and services that could be found within their neighborhood or local area. In 2010, the percentage of consumers using the Internet to make local purchasing decisions grew to 97 percent, with the definition of local being within a 15-mile radius. Now, with the advent of smart phones and GPS locators, searches for businesses within a six-mile radius have also become common, especially when people are on the road. If you believe your business doesn't need an Internet presence because you draw your customers from a five- or 10-mile radius, you are effectively closing off an entire qualified market seeking your business online.

A Vet's Sure Bet

An office manager of a neighborhood veterinary hospital was seeking ways to cut costs and more effectively market the animal clinic. By analyzing expenses, she discovered the company was spending more than $2,000 per month on Yellow Pages and phone book advertising. Further investigation showed that more new patients came in from word-of-mouth referrals than any other source. It was clear that phone book advertising was not a good investment as its cost was not being covered by the revenue it generated. *Realizing that families were primarily using the Internet for information on pet care needs, the office manager was convinced this was where the budget needed to shift. She discontinued numerous phone book placements over the course of the first three months, reducing the cost by $1,000 a month. At a cost of $200 per month, she found a search engine optimization company to help the clinic implement a targeted local online program. The optimization focused on attracting pet owners living within a 20-mile radius of the clinic who were seeking information online about pet care. Within three months of its implementation, the online program generated a double-digit increase in monthly income. Coupons and special programs were added to their online presence, along with a LinkedIn and Facebook page with links to the website. Within one week of launching a Fan Page, 188 fans had joined. The clinic also added a pet fitness center section to their website in conjunction with a Biggest Loser contest to bring attention to pet obesity. Ten pets were chosen, nine dogs and one cat, from photos and information posted to the website by pet owners. Overweight pets were initially screened, weighed and given blood tests at the beginning of the three-month program. Staff members served as mentors to pets and their owners, tracking each pet's progress, which was posted on the website and linked to other social media pages for fans and visitors to view. Purina and numerous other sponsors participated by contributing to a grand prize that included a year's worth of pet food for the pet that lost the biggest percentage of*

> **I have been steering clients away from ads in phone books to other marketing initiatives since the early 1990s. When the Internet began to prove its worth and value, companies began realizing greater returns from leveraging search engine optimization at a fraction of the cost of phone book advertising.**

body weight. While other veterinary practices and clinics were seeing a decline in pet visits, which meant eliminating staff positions, the online efforts of this clinic led to it seeing an average of 25 new clients a month. Twelve months after launching the program, the clinic saw their website activity grow from less than 200 hits a month to several thousand. By this time, they had successfully reduced phone book advertising by an additional $500 a month for a total savings of $1,500 while realizing a steady double-digit increase in monthly income since the program was launched.

The Age Myth: Are you a business targeting the senior market? Do you believe that these individuals are steadfast phone book users? Think again. According to a generational study on Internet usage, usage is growing fastest among those aged 70 and above. They are using the Internet for e-mail, online searches and research about health issues. Internet users ages 65 and older have tripled their use of high-speed Internet access. Assuming they only have dial-up is another misperception.

The At Work, No Play Myth: In a study conducted by WebTrends, 93 percent of office workers admit they conduct personal business online while at work. In other words, everything from paying bills to booking personal travel plans is occurring on the job. With this in mind, I reiterate the cautionary note I mentioned in Secret #28. Be careful about using Flash with sound upon entry to your website, especially if you offer a personal or consumer service or product. A worker who clicks to your site out of curiosity will click away just as fast if a sound track starts blaring when he or she is supposed to be finishing a report.

Search-ability Cost Myth: A 2010 benchmark study indicated that the quality of sales leads generated by organic searches were two times more qualified than those generated by paid search ads. Understanding the protocol in which search engines seek out their listings will enable organic search success. Your homepage is the entry portal for search engines seeking websites. But other aspects of your site will also attract them as they seek out current information. Therefore, news articles, blogs and any place you frequently update will give your site a higher ranking. Making sure your homepage has feeds from frequently updated areas of your site is a smart strategy.

There are some basic low- or no-cost actions you can take to increase your presence on the Internet. One is posting your business, location, phone number and website address on Google Map, Yahoo Map and other map locator sources. Indexing your website's site map to Google, Yahoo and other search engines is also something most businesses do not know how to do, yet can be easily done with a sitemap generator. A free resource is www.xml-sitemap.com.

Indexing your site map helps the search engines prioritize and know that your site exists in the system sooner with more targeted results.

The best news for small business regarding search engine optimization (SEO) is that there are companies with documented success rates that specialize in localized optimization for businesses at a fraction of the cost of phone book advertising or other optimization services. This means you only pay for targeting users seeking businesses in your market concentration within a designated geographic area. One such company that has produced phenomenal results specifically for small businesses is AdzZoo.

•   •   •

As you have probably surmised, growth companies understand that being on the Internet has replaced being in the phone book. While telecommunications is attempting to catch up with online listings, the same money can be spent in organic and targeted optimization that works better than any online phone directory. Make optimization a part of your Internet game plan to hear your phone ring more and to see your e-mail inbox get fuller — by leaps and bounds.

STRATEGIC
INVOLVEMENTS

31

Purposeful Affiliation

Bootstrapping small companies know it's good business to get involved in the communities where they are located and in the marketplace they serve. It demonstrates that the company is vested in the community and in the marketplace. However, many business owners do not undertake these initiatives strategically. This results in a great deal of effort without much return on their investment of time and money. In the research my firm conducted, we found high-growth business owners were involved at the board or committee level with an average of two or three organizations. Their employees were also encouraged to get involved in organizations so the company could be well represented in several different areas.

So what was the difference between how successful business owners approached being involved compared to others? These savvy marketers understood that volunteer activities should be logical components of their marketing and operational strategy. Their first step was to identify the organizations that best met their marketing goals.

To help you make better choices, an organization should fall into at least one of three categories: 1) It puts you in direct contact with your target market; 2) It puts you in contact with those who can refer you to your ideal target market; or 3) It provides resources or business support that will help you more effectively operate your business.

Direct Contact with Ideal Target Market: Does the organization put you in direct contact with people you want as customers? Do you have a clear understanding of who your ideal target market is? If not, revisit Secret # 13. Knowing your target markets and the types of organizations they participate in will let you easily identify civic groups, charities and community and business organizations where qualified prospects are involved.

Contact with Strong Referral Base: Another good choice is to become involved in organizations where members can refer you to your ideal market. These can include a referral networking group where members meet regularly to provide qualified referrals to one another. Visit several to make sure the group is committed to ensuring members understand each other's ideal markets. You don't want to be part of a group where people just supply each other names. Also consider other professional groups that may serve your ideal customer in other ways. These groups often offer sponsorships or affiliate/associate memberships to those serving the same market. It's a means of building resources and support within the group.

Operational Resource and Support: Business owners should never underestimate the value of being involved in groups that offer resources and support that can make their business better. Successful owners realize they need to be in a continuous learning mode when it comes to their business. They constantly seek out opportunities for gaining insight, knowledge, support and resources. Examples include trade associations, chambers of commerce and professional business organizations.

Golden Connections

A consultant who focused on one key client realized after 10 years that her business model could not be sustainable for growth. Having witnessed a family member build a business over a lifetime that could not be sold for any real value, she knew there was a void in the marketplace that needed to be filled. Seeing the need for someone who could help business owners understand and build real value in their enterprises, she decided to shift her business focus. With this new business focus and model in mind, she relocated to an area where entrepreneurship was a hotbed, even though she knew she was starting at ground zero. She hired a marketing consultant in 2006 and over the next two years implemented her plan to build a brand and platform for her business. The key to her strategy was affiliating with key organizations that effectively connected her with her target market and created credibility and awareness for her business. Seeking to specifically aid women entrepreneurs in succession

> *In our study, more than 60 percent of growth companies had a defined action plan for strategic involvements with civic, charitable, professional and industry groups that placed owners and employees in direct contact with the company's ideal target markets.*

planning, she became involved in eWomenNetwork, the National Association of Women Business Owners and the Women's Professional Organization. Each one brought her face-to-face with women business owners at various stages of their business. She also wanted to build connections on the economic and government side of the marketplace so she sought and received an appointment to the local government's women's advisory board. Forming numerous strategic partnerships to provide an entire entourage of experts for her clients to resource was an ongoing process. Because her business focused on client companies' financial success and financial planners also targeted women entrepreneurs, she became a member of the local Financial Planners Association. She eventually became one of the chapter's few women board members. An Asian American, she also became involved with two charitable organizations that were especially meaningful to her. She contributed money, expertise and time. She then expanded her reach to the national level by writing white papers and submitting them to organizations for publication and by pursuing speaking engagements in front of her targeted audience. This gave her national media exposure. By choosing her involvements based on a strategic plan, she continued to build one connection on another. She proved that when you do anything with purpose and focus, the outcome is solid gold. She is now a columnist for Women Entrepreneur magazine, has recently published a book and is considered a leading authority on succession planning for women-owned businesses. Her efforts have paid off with double-digit annual growth and double-digit profitability.

Now that you understand the three primary reasons to be involved in a group, you can make better choices moving forward. However, this is only the starting point. You must also understand the different levels of involvement so you can achieve the highest return on your investments.

Member: As a member of a group you probably paid dues or a fee to join. Or you may have simply signed up to receive information. This means you are only taking advantage of the group at the most basic level. If the information is of value in running your business or elevates your knowledge base, this is perfectly fine. Continually evaluate the value of the information and how often you use it.

Participant: At this level, you are physically engaged in the group by regularly attending its meetings or events. In most cases, these are events you personally attend, although online events are gaining momentum. This trend will change group participation in ways yet to be comprehended. For now, consider how you participate in the groups where you are a member. If all you do is show up and gather a few business cards, take a step back. Evaluate the group from the three criteria discussed earlier. If it falls within any of them, consider increasing your participation in ways that create more value for you and the organization.

Involved: This scenario has likely happened to you. You joined an organization and participated by attending some of its events. Then a board member or committee chair personally asked you to become more involved in a particular area. You said yes, and you became involved.

Strategically Involved: Growth-oriented business owners understand the importance of being strategically involved. How is this different from just being involved? When you have a strategic plan, you have defined not only the types of organizations you will be involved in, but also *how* you will be involved – all based on how it supports your business growth. You have both a long-term and short-term plan strategy that defines how both the group and your business will benefit. All too often business owners let an organization's representative dictate how they get involved. They just said "yes" without considering why and how it made sense for their companies' goals and objectives.

Many business owners I have worked with think they don't have the time to be strategically involved in an organization. The good news is there are numerous ways to accomplish it. Some options are short-term while others require a long-term commitment. The key is to identify how you can best contribute based on how you are strategically growing your business. By understanding the simple connection between your strategy and what the organization hopes to achieve, you can create a win-win situation every time.

Remember that each involvement should help you achieve your goals by putting you in direct contact with your ideal target market or those who can refer you to it, or to help you gain support or resources to grow your business. You also want to identify areas that will bring attention to your strengths and abilities so others can witness what you are capable of doing. Those who can be counted on in a volunteer capacity are viewed as ideal to do business with because of their integrity and ability to get things done.

Take some initial time at the participant level within an organization to gauge the different opportunities for involvement. Talk to other members who have been involved in areas you have interest to gain insights into time commitments and expectations.

- <u>Committee Level</u>: Identify a committee that uses your talents in the best way for the organization. This is a good first step that doesn't create an extensive time commitment. You are part of group where each member is assigned one task within a larger effort.

- <u>Special Projects</u>: Sometimes the best way to stand out is to take charge of projects no one else is willing to take on. If it is a short-term project, you will have the ability to tackle the project and get it done without it being a burden over time. If it requires a long-term commitment, offer to oversee a first phase and then build a committee where another person is your successor. In one instance, a banking director volunteered to oversee the establishment of a charitable foundation within an organization. She researched the proper procedure, and another volunteer stepped forward to get the foundation established.

- <u>Committee Chair</u>: Stepping up to chair a committee will place you in a leadership role. The key to being an effective chairperson is assembling a strong committee to support you. This is important for three reasons. First, it means you aren't a committee of one doing everything and thereby overburdening yourself. Second, you are connecting with people who are ideally interested in helping and supporting the committee's success. So you'll make connections for your business as well. Third, you can assess the group of committee members to identify your successor.

- <u>Board Member</u>: Depending on the structure of the organization, there are three levels of board involvement. One type is a volunteer board that is responsible for leading, setting policies and rolling up their sleeves and doing the actual work. Typically the organization does not have paid staff and requires a volunteer board to get things done. This level will require more time on your part. A second type is a governing board. This type of board sets policies and oversees volunteer committees. It does not require as much hands-on involvement. You are serving in a leadership and policy-making capacity. This organization has paid staff supporting it operationally and administratively. The third type is an advisory board, which typically supports a governing or volunteer board. It usually requires a smaller time commitment, but you are expected to provide a high level of guidance and expertise to assist the board in special initiatives or circumstances.

Strategically Better

The co-owner of a language services firm was a committee member for an organization's gala awards event. In the midst of its planning, an unexpected situation arose that meant a new chairperson had to step forward and take over the leadership for the event. She was happy to step into the role and the event was a huge success. As a result of her ability to take over and lead under difficult circumstances, she was invited to join the board to oversee all of the group's special events.

However, in reviewing her strategic plan, this was not the best choice. Her marketing consultant steered her toward volunteering for another position on the board that focused on public policy at the federal level. One of the main focuses of this group's public policy initiatives was increasing opportunities for government contracting. This was a more strategic involvement for her because her plans for her business included securing large government contracts. The position would give her valuable first-hand insight as well as help the board fill a position that was typically difficult to fill. She was able to easily recommend a gala committee member for the special events board position. Today her double-digit growth company is certified as a women business enterprise, a minority business enterprise and is winning government and private contracts at the local, state and national levels.

Over-Involved: In the study we conducted comparing growth companies to stagnant or negative-growth ones, business owners of growing companies were strategically involved in two to three organizations. In addition, growth companies also encouraged and supported employees to be strategically involved. However, in many of my marketing workshops or small business center courses I have taught, owners typically tell me they aren't involved in any organizations at all. Neither are their employees. It's easy to understand that not being involved in any organizations can be detrimental and contribute to stagnant growth. But in our research, we made a surprising discovery. Negative growth or no-growth companies were actually over-involved. The owners had commitments to five or more organizations. These business owners were literally volunteering their time and profits away under the belief that "getting out there" would help build the company during though times. In many cases, only the business owner was involved not any of the employees, which meant the key person to run the company was being distracted affecting operations as well This is why being strategically involved is so important.

• • •

Review your current involvements and assess them with this new understanding. Transform your volunteer commitments so they create the highest return on your investment of time, talent and money. Making sure you and your employees are involved in the right organizations in the right way will prove immensely valuable to your bottom line.

32

Trade Collaborations

If you think it's a waste of time to be involved in a group where it's likely you'll rub a lot of elbows with your competition, think again. Your narrow mindedness is probably costing you business, hurting your reputation and losing you opportunities to grow your business. In our CRISP Principle research, we found growth companies were involved in professional trade groups at the local, regional and national levels to support their industry and gain insight and connections to help grow their businesses. In some cases, the business owner was involved, and other times it was an employee.

Professional Trade Associations: Belonging to an industry trade association brings you a wealth of information, best practices and potential joint and employer opportunities. When you take the involvement to a strategic level where you are on a committee or in a leadership role helping to set policies, you elevate your stature in your industry and are recognized as one who genuinely cares about it. It is also an ideal way to get to know and keep a pulse on your competition. This can allow you to identify potential partners and threats in order to make better strategic decisions for your company.

Peer & User Groups: Professional trade associations often offer peer, user and special interest groups to bring together people in specialized disciplines to share ideas and solutions to common problems. Popular within the technology industry, these groups have proven valuable to increasing employees' skill sets simply by interacting with peers in a non-threatening environment. Savvy growth-minded IT project management companies have also found peer groups an excellent way to gain additional specialists for client project work.

Joint Ventures & Collaborations: Trade association involvements put you in direct contact with those in the same industry including both competitors and non-competitors. We spoke about competitor collaborations in Secret #23. Non-competitors within your industry are ideal partners to collaborate with on a variety of levels. Take a look at businesses in your trade groups and identify those that offer complementary services and products to the same target market. From cross promotions (Secret #24) to strategic alliances (Secret #35), there are a number of ways to build a solid base of opportunities through these connections. Another smart practice is conducting a joint meeting where you bring customers together for a social or business meeting or function.

Showing Up

The owners of a specialty dental surgical equipment manufacturing company knew that success in business starts with being smart in business. They also knew that business was first and foremost about building and solidifying relationships. So while larger competitors sent regional representatives to national shows, this company sent their entire team. Their mantra was that although you can fake caring and being interested, you cannot fake showing up. The company commits people and resources to 14 major trade shows each year, and they do more than show up. They sponsor over 240 surgical courses a year in the United States and Canada, and manage the entire process for their dental practice clients including a 50,000-member contact mailing list, enrolling doctors in specialized courses and identifying specialized procedures needed to further advance skills. Collaborating with others in their industry is a regular practice. Because they made everything for dental implants except the implants, they coordinated dinner meetings among their best clients and those of an implant producer. About 15 to 30 customers sat around the table during these dinners as the two companies expressed their gratitude, gained valuable feedback and enjoyed the company of colleagues. The emphasis was on cultivating relationships and building friendships, not pushing products. They knew these customers were already sold on their companies, so it was about

> **Growth companies are three times more likely to be involved in their professional trade associations than companies with negative or stagnant growth. Further exploration of this statistic validates that those who are considered respected in their industry are viewed as a better company to do business with.**

nurturing the relationships and affirming they were companies that cared. As a matter of fact, the company cared so much that it offered support and programs no others were offering. A four-day internship program was offered to the children of their dental clients. The program provided interviewing and presentation skills training to college students. Named among the top entrepreneurial companies in its region and considered a leader in its industry with double-digit growth, this company proves that when you show how much you care, it pays.

Industry Masterminds: Companies across the country are identifying similar non-competing businesses within their industry to form mastermind advisory groups to share best practices and knowledge so all of them can grow. They typically meet in a retreat-style setting on a quarterly basis in a central location around the country – or at each other's sites – to learn how each of them approaches their business. These groups have proven especially beneficial in identifying trends and anticipating shifts. They are usually most effective for companies seeking to stay regional or local in scope. They also provide opportunities where another firm's expertise can be tapped or resourced to create a new stream of income.

Public Policy Groups: Government legislation today impacts every industry. Growth-oriented entrepreneurs understand the necessity to stay on top of pending legislation so they can anticipate its effects on their industry, customers, and business. Most trade associations have a public policy arm that performs this function. Some also have political action committees that lobby and get involved in elections on a local, state or federal level. The value in this extends to your clients as you can inform them via legislative alerts about laws that could affect their business. This action can help you stand out from competitors who are not keeping a pulse on these situations. Some companies have begun advocacy groups to tackle a particular industry-wide issue. For example, a group of non-medical in-home service providers formed an advocacy group to lobby at the state level regarding Medicare and co-pay premiums.

•　　•　　•

The value of being involved in trade associations and industry groups cannot be overstated. First consider the ways you can be involved locally and then go from there. As stated in Secret #23, knowing your competition is not only good for business, but also knowing key players within your industry and being one yourself is good for business growth.

33

Charitable Giving

If you have put charitable giving on hold because you think you need to focus on building your business first, get out of that mindset now. Growth-minded entrepreneurs make charitable giving a part of their business practices from the start. Then, as their companies grow, their charitable efforts grow as well. In the CRISP Principle research study, we found that when you consider companies donating time, talent, services, goods or money, nearly 85 percent incorporated some form of charitable giving into their operations.

Donating Time & Talent: If you can afford to give time more than money, why are you hesitating? Any director of a nonprofit charitable organization will quickly tell you how valuable a business owner's time and talent is to their organization. Small businesses, like nonprofits, must be especially resourceful to make money and resources go further. A small business owner or a key employee assisting a nonprofit provides a gold mine of insights on how to do more with less. Entrepreneurial company representatives are also generally more hands-on and willing to lend a hand on volunteer boards and committees because of their can-do attitude and approach to business. They are likely to shift to areas where needed because being agile and adaptable is the way they do business. These are abilities much in demand at nonprofits.

Donating Goods & Services: Another way you can make a difference is by donating services or goods. However, be careful to budget for this just as you would budget for anything in your business. Generous entrepreneurs have gotten themselves into trouble by giving away goods or services to the point of negatively impacting their income statements. Determine an overall value of services and goods you will allocate for charitable giving and stick to it. Just because someone asks it doesn't mean you have to say yes. Develop policies that identify where donations will be given. Get clients and employees involved in the process to bring a true team passion around the spirit of making a difference.

You also need to understand how the IRS views donated services and goods. It is favorable for products-oriented businesses and unfavorable for services-oriented ones. Donated products can be written off as a charitable donation with a tangible bill of goods value receipt and a written acceptance of receipt from the charitable organization.

However, the IRS views services as too variable in how they are priced, and so they cannot be written off as a charitable contribution, but it is a business expense. Unfair, I know. We can thank unscrupulous owners in services industries who inflated the value of what they donated for this situation.

However, there are ways you can leverage donating services as a win-win for your business and the charitable organization. Negotiate your service donation in conjunction with being named an in-kind partner or special contributor to gain promotional value. For instance, when my firm donated its services to design a unique invitation for an organization's annual awards program, we exchanged it for a corporate table where I invited clients and staff. My company was also named in the program and on the invitation.

Be sure the entity understands the dollar value of your donated service in the marketplace. They often have no idea of what they are getting for nothing. This will allow you to make a difference for them while also leveraging the donation for your business when you can't write it off.

Bountiful Giving

When the founder of a managed networking and voiceover Internet company established his business in 2004, he knew that his business was going to be much more than an employer. He envisioned a company that would embrace the energy that exists within a community with a focus on being of service as much as providing a service. He considered his company's profits a means of harvesting monies for charitable giving supported by a willing workforce committed to making a difference as well. By serving the communities in its market area, the founder felt his company would better serve its customers in a way that would resonate and touch lives. Therefore, the company made charitable giving a planned budgeted component of the company's operational capital and an

> *In our study, 81 percent of business owners in growth companies were involved on a charitable board or committee and 77 percent set aside a budget for charitable contributions. While the assumption is only big business gives to charities, small businesses are a valued philanthropic force.*

underlying driving force within the company culture.
The job of monitoring charitable giving was considered
so important it was assigned to the vice president of
finance. Employees served as key identifiers of charitable
causes and organizations to support financially and with
in-kind support. This included children's athletic
leagues and families in crisis that needed a helping
hand. Whether contributing in-kind installations and
goods to the National Wildlife Federation, sponsoring
events to raise money for developmentally disabled
adults, or contributing funds and manpower to refurbish
public school facilities and grounds, this entrepreneur
and his group of passionate employees have understood
the true power of giving. With an unprecedented 20-25
percent of net profits being donated to worthy causes
annually (compared to the standard 5 percent), the
company realized a nearly 3,000 percent growth rate in
four years and proved that doing business with giving in
mind is also good for the bottom line.

Donating Money: You may be hesitant to give money to charities because you think it needs to be a significant amount. This is another incorrect assumption. In our CRISP Principle study, we found that growth companies' monetary contributions to charity ranged from a few hundred to several thousand dollars a year. It was evident they had determined what they could give and then stayed within those parameters. Another practice among these companies was not giving all their budgeted dollars to one charity. Instead they spread it around to help a number of entities. This held true even for those with only a few hundred dollars to give. For example, one business with $500 budgeted for charitable giving donated to 12 different organizations at $25, $50 and $100 levels. Whether it was Thanksgiving baskets to needy families or funds for book scholarships, the company realized its money was valued even in small increments.

•   •   •

People like to do business with companies who care for more than their own bottom line. Companies that "do good" make the markets they serve feel good. And that's good for everyone concerned.

34

Charitable Cause

Business owners are passionate by nature. So they are often passionate about making a difference based on their own personal values. These values are likely shared with their employees and customers, so a decision to support a particular cause is the best way to funnel the business's charitable resources. If this is the direction you want your business to take, you need to identify the cause and determine your level of commitment. Some companies adopt multiple causes at different commitment levels.

Identifying a Cause: The place to start is where you personally want to make a difference. Don't choose a cause just because it will make you or your business look good. Choose a cause you truly care about. Get your employees and even their families involved in developing a list for consideration. Once you have narrowed down possible beneficiaries, reach out to your customer base for more insight. If you are practicing Secret #13, you already have a sense of the charitable causes your customer base is likely to support. This creates a win-win. Going back to the definition that strategic involvements are ones where you are involved in the right organizations for the right reasons, choose one that you and your customers are passionate, connecting you with your ideal target market

Extreme Caring

A Northwest-based consulting group delivering business, technology and staffing solutions was primed from the start to be of service far beyond its core offerings. That's because its co-founders believed that supporting those in need was just a natural way to be. Giving to worthy causes was simply an extension of who they were. There was great gratification in seeing the direct impact the contributions had on charities and the people they served. The company's list of causes it supports is extensive because its employees are as involved in the giving decisions as the founders. The company set up a

501(c)3 charitable foundation dedicating $100,000 per year for employees to determine how the money is allocated for charitable purposes, while picking up any expenses so the full amount of the commitment could make a difference. At any given time, more than 25 organizations reap the benefits of the company's generosity. Personal connections are always a key factor in choosing a particular cause to support. Special circumstances can also dictate decisions. In one instance, an employee whose husband had passed away was given funds for two years of college for her two daughters. The company's 250-plus employees and founders also personally give to a variety of causes in 21 states. Named among Washington's Top 25 Philanthropic Medium-sized Companies, the business also grew revenues from $673,562 to $27 million in four years. This consulting group proves that extreme caring is extremely rewarding for everyone concerned.

Adopting a Cause: After you identify a particular cause to support, you need to budget your resources to do it. Contact the charity to make its leadership aware of your plans and arrange a meeting. This will familiarize you with the organization's greatest needs so you can effectively plug your company's resources where they can have the biggest impact. Be sure to do it based on your business competencies and resources. Events or projects the organization had wanted to launch, but had no support for may now be able to get off the ground with your help. Your company can be the catalyst to make it happen. Once your level of commitment is defined by you, it is time to develop a plan and budget around the effort so everyone is on the same page. This plan and budget should be shared with employees and the key leadership of the organization. When you adopt a charity and make commitments to it, it is no different than serving a customer. Do not fall victim to the mindset that charitable efforts can be put on hold whenever customer demand picks up. I can't understate the damage it will do to your

Growth companies care and it shows. In the CRISP Principle study, more than 60 percent adopted a specific cause to support. Selection of the charitable cause was based on a combination of the owner's interests with employee and customer preferences.

reputation if you don't fulfill a charitable commitment. This is why having a plan that everyone understands and has bought into is crucial. Managing expectations on the charitable front is no different than managing expectations in a client relationship.

Managing Multiple Causes: You may choose to adopt several causes. Some may be given services or goods, others time and talent, and still others monetary support. The criteria for choosing several causes is no different from choosing one. However, to properly manage the effort, it is even more important to have an overall budget that considers all your resources. Don't forget the statistic shared in Secret #31 about over-involvement literally consuming a company's ability to be profitable. Don't give more than you can afford.

•   •   •

How you make a difference is up to you. The key is to always have in mind the best interests of everyone being served. If you begin doing it for selfish reasons, it is time to step back. Remind yourself – and others – how fortunate the company is to have business, especially when others are struggling.

35

Strategic Relationships

Business owners who understand they are never alone also understand the business-building power of joining forces with others. High-growth companies make developing and fostering strategic relationships a way of doing business on several levels.

Business Alliances: Identifying other companies to align with to go after a larger piece of business or better serve your market is a reason to consider forming a strategic alliance. Some alliances help provide an area of expertise to compliment the other company's capabilities while another alliance is formed to help a business expand into new markets. Growth companies understand the value of forming both non-competitive alliances and competitive alliances. A non-competitive alliance is with a company going after the same market profile, but not a competitor. These companies offer either complimentary services or products that dovetail into an opportunity to serve each of your client bases jointly more effectively. For instance, a software development company joins forces with a computer training company in order to provide a turnkey installation and training program to clients.

A competitive alliance is a strategic partnership formed with either a direct or indirect competitor. During a down economy, competitors aligning to get more business together may seem contradictory when opportunities are shrinking at the same time. However, big businesses are cutting staff and opening a window of opportunity for smaller competing businesses that join together to go after larger contracts offering a higher caliber team overseeing the project. In addition, government spending also increases during down economic times, opening up more local, state and federal contracting opportunities.

Unite & Conquer

By looking at ebbs and flows in design work demand, an architect knew from experience that the health of his industry was the first indicator that a downturn was coming in the construction industry. Therefore, he decided that when he started his own firm, it would grow by serving a diverse industry base and providing broad service offerings to shield his firm from the roller coaster ride he had seen others in his field endure. As market demand shifted, his firm was able to shift along with it because he never had all his eggs in one basket. When indicators of the slowing economy began to appear in late 2007 and early 2008, his firm was ready to proactively shift focus to where opportunities were still strong, such as government contracts and institutional work. Since the firm had gained a reputation as an expert in green and sustainable design, they were able to leverage this expertise with government and institutional opportunities seeking this expertise. The architect also saw opportunities to team with competitors to win government and private contracts that were bigger in scope. As an example, his architectural firm took the lead in a project with its expertise in utility operations design and overall project management while bringing in a direct competitor with a specialized engineering capability. Valuing his own client relationships, he deemed a respected competitor's track record with a client as an opportunity to grow together by enhancing its capability with his firm's specialized expertise. Reciprocally, competitors with an expertise his firm did not possess teamed up to enhance its ability to serve loyal clients. Although the architectural industry was taking its biggest hit in decades as a result of the recession that began in 2008, this architectural powerhouse saw double-digit growth and was named among the 50 fastest growing companies in its market in 2009.

> **Nearly 50 percent of growth companies in the CRISP Principle research formed strategic alliances with competitors as a means of growing sales through obtaining larger contracts as a partnering team. Seven out of 10 growth companies also formed strategic alliances with non-competing companies.**

Advisory Boards: Another way to gain insight and perspective to make better decisions to grow your company – especially during challenging times – is to identify individuals who will join an advisory board to mentor you. These advisory board members may be semi-retired or retired professionals from your industry, suppliers and even longtime customers. Meeting on a semi-annual or quarterly basis, this approach gives the business owner the ability to use the group as a sounding board for ideas, challenges or strategy development.

Mastermind Groups: Growth-minded business owners also leverage strategic relationships by forming mastermind groups. These are formed specifically for the purpose of gaining insights and operational advice from other business owners in other industries. Meeting on a monthly or bi-monthly basis for a period of several months to several years, the group is typically small with about six to eight members. A two-hour meeting allows each member to share any challenges and offer advice and guidance to one another. Each meeting typically focuses on a particular topic or theme based on the group's mutual concerns and areas where they want to improve. These groups are priceless for the out-of-box thinking they can generate by applying concepts from one industry to another.

Universities: Colleges, universities and technical institutes offer numerous opportunities for small businesses to leverage strategic relationships. By teaching at a community college or university for evening or corporate and continuing education classes, you can add credibility and exposure for your business. Using interns and participating in work-study programs not only support your business, but can be beneficial by expanding your circle of influential relationships. Those running these programs are continually out in the community. Some small businesses conduct joint research and product development initiatives with universities and local institutions at a fraction of the cost of doing it in-house.

•   •   •

Take a look around you. Consider how your business can build strategic relationships that can help take your business to the next level. Start by looking at those in your existing referral network base and explore the possibilities.

36
Sponsorships

You always want your business to stand out from your competitors. It's a goal you never want to forget. For growth-minded small businesses, it means your marketing-dollar expenditures need to create the biggest bang for the buck. Growth companies choose sponsorships over ads for a variety of reasons and with very clear expectations. When growth companies select one particular sponsorship, it's because they view it as promotional partnership where both gain value from the relationship.

In-kind vs. Cash: Offering goods or services in exchange for an in-kind partnership has proven highly effective for growth companies. But for it to be successful, your negotiations must be based on real dollar-for-dollar value. You must reach an agreement on how the business will gain exposure and how the group will benefit. Start by looking at the budget for the program or event. Being able to offer a product or service that takes the program or event to a higher level is one value your can bring. Being able to offer in-kind products or services that were originally budgeted to help the organization's cash flow is also an excellent way to appeal to the group. As a result, they gain a valuable in-kind offer and you gain a higher level of exposure.

A Cut Above

A photography studio provided in-kind photography and production for a PowerPoint presentation with an audio soundtrack for an organization's awards event. In exchange, the photographer was able to sell prints to attendees and shared a portion of the proceeds with the group. The photographer was allowed to distribute promotional material plus received recognition and exposure before and after the event when people went online to view and order prints. A florist provided creative centerpieces for the tables at the same event. The arrangements were designed to be easily divided so everyone at the table could take home a prize. In essence, this made everyone at the event a winner. In both cases, these in-kind partnerships took the event to a higher level in the eyes of attendees. They also increased exposure for the businesses before, during and after the event.

Long-term vs. Short-term: Growth companies prefer sponsorships that offer exposure over a period of time rather than a one-time event. That makes sponsorships with extended periods of exposure more appealing than those offering it just immediately before and during an event. Companies also prefer to be an exclusive partner over a period of two to three years to prevent a competitor from sponsoring the event. Look for events that promise exposure and recognition for your company on an extended basis rather than only in conjunction with the event.

Programs vs. Events: Growth-minded businesses also prefer to support programs that offer a series of events. For instance, a consulting business sponsored a chamber of commerce's four-part workshop series targeted to small and mid-market businesses. The events focused on four different areas of best practices and featured panels moderated by consultants from the sponsoring firm.

Compared to stagnant or no-growth companies, growth companies were twice as likely to be an event sponsor and three times more likely to become a sponsor that promised year-long or multiple year exposure. These companies also preferred to be viewed as partners versus sponsors.

Offering Sponsorships: You may want to consider offering sponsorships as a way to create another stream of income. While building credibility for the business, it also brings value with highly-targeted exposure for the partners who participate. An employee assessment and leadership development company established a members-only success institute that featured five meetings a year for business owners, CEOs and executives to share best practices. A sponsor was secured for the meeting location and other sponsors covered the cost of the breakfast, materials and guest speakers. A media production company specializing in eco-content for print, Internet and TV, leveraged an individual promotional partnership for a long-term, six-figure deal with a large regional grocery store chain. The partnership made it the exclusive provider of focused everyday green living information and tips for families in the chain's website and in-store promotions.

• • •

The underlying success factor in all these sponsorships is that value is perceived beyond the amount invested. Not only are you receiving value, but you are giving value to the partner organization. One-shot promotional deals should be dismissed for others offering more depth, reach and exposure over time.

37

A Sense of Community

Tragedies that touch the hearts of millions have made people realize how precious life and the communities they live in truly are. From 9-11 to Hurricane Katrina to earthquake-ravaged Haiti, we were all reminded of what can be accomplished when a community pulls together in times of need. We also realized we can make a difference, even in small ways, to make communities where we live and work better places. Growth-oriented small businesses embrace this concept of community service and incorporate it into how they operate.

Corporate Citizenship: Growth companies realize that to be valued in a community, they need to give value beyond the services or products they sell. They also need to make a conscientious effort to truly become part of their community. Being a corporate citizen is the goal – not just being a corporation located within a city or rural limits. It means working in tangible ways to help enhance and improve the community.

Community First

A young and determined insurance agent bought a stagnating franchise in 2006. With a strong belief that people do business with people who care about their community, she focused on building a relationship-based business where community involvement was at the forefront. She demonstrated through actions, not just words, how much she appreciated and valued the community. Her firm sponsored a Mother's Day essay contest, hosted child safety-seat inspections twice a year, provided seminars for first-time homebuyers and gave talks to high school driver education classes. She hosted programs such as "Strapped for Cash" during National Teen Driver Safety Week, which gave cash to students found wearing their seatbelts while driving off school grounds. She sponsored a food drive, using her office as a drop-off point, and also hosted an annual community day with games, food and prizes. She designated excess green space behind her building as a community space for dog walking and Saturday flag football tournaments. In addition, she gave employees paid time off to help volunteer and build a Habitat for Humanity home. The efforts of this community-minded business owner were rewarded by a community that embraced her business. In just three years, it grew from insuring 1,532 households to 1,957 and achieved a retention rate of over 90 percent. In 2009, her firm was rated as a top business leader by a regional business magazine, the number-one health insurance agency in North Carolina and 75th in the country among her franchise's 17,000 agents across the country.

Involving Employees: To be viewed as a genuine corporate citizen, it is crucial for companies to support their employees' community activities. Find ways to participate within the community on a personal level and as a group. Employees are more likely to participate in community activities on behalf of their company if it is also meaningful to them on a personal level.

Growth-oriented business owners understand the value and importance of offering encouragement and support to employees being involved in their communities with more than 70 percent of growth companies making its community involvement a company-wide practice.

Small Ways, Big Impact: Sometimes the best ways to make a difference in a community are through small and manageable ways. Here are some ideas you can easily adapt and incorporate into your community service plan. You may want to involve staff and commit resources to a different community activity each month. Consider selecting activities that can re-occur year after year as a part of your community outreach.

- Be a drop-off location for a clothing, toy or food drive
- Host a Scout troop visit to help them earn a badge or designation
- Sponsor a family in need over the holidays
- Support church or youth group functions

- Support youth sports teams
- Support employees in PTA or church activities
- Adopt an area school and donate supplies or tutor students

There are numerous other opportunities, but this listing gives you some ideas. Your employees and customers can help you identify a list from which you can prioritize and choose.

•　　•　　•

The ways your business can be active in the community are only limited by your time and interest. In addition to involving your employees, ask your customers where they see the greatest community need and make it a team effort that includes them as well.

PUBLIC RELATIONS

38

Proactive Pursuit

One of the most cost effective and credible ways to promote your business and reinforce your company image is through regular publicity. The problem is that most business owners don't understand how to get started or have misconceptions about what public relations entails. I am surprised by the number of business owners who believe companies pay newspapers to run feature stories or that they have to pay a fee to get their announcements printed. After conducting my CRISP Principle study, I decided a public relations training seminar would be one of the first training workshops I'd offer. High-growth companies were implementing multi-faceted public relations efforts as part of their core marketing initiatives. I was committed to helping business owners who could not afford a PR firm learn how to do it themselves. I didn't want the fact that they could not afford outside help to keep them from adding this powerful component to their overall marketing plan.

When I work with a company that has been relying on advertising for promotion, I often advise them to stop placing ads and focus on an aggressive media relations program instead. About three to six months later, we review the need for ads. Typically, we find advertising is no longer necessary or only needs to be highly selective as the PR efforts are generating excellent results. We also find that any select placements get better results than the multiple placements previously garnered. Why? Because people will notice an ad more if they have heard about the company in other places, especially by reading an article.

A PR program helps businesses meet a multitude of objectives: creating awareness of the company in the marketplace, enhancing its credibility and image, increasing referrals and the effectiveness of its sales efforts, and helping reduce other marketing expenditures such as ads. In this secret, we will discuss the media relations aspect of PR, specifically focusing on its basic component — sending out regular news releases.

Sending News Releases: The key to getting your company mentioned in newspapers and on TV or radio is sending regular information to media contacts. Distributing news to the media is as much about making them aware of your business as it is hoping they will publish the information. You are working to develop an ongoing communications relationship with them.

Understanding this is critical to getting your news published on a regular basis. The most effective way to build strong media relationships is to feed media contacts regular news tidbits through news releases. I like to call news releases "love letters to the media." You must prepare them in a way the media contacts will respect, appreciate and eventually disseminate because they like what they see. Your news release also regularly reminds them you are in the marketplace and available as a resource. As releases are received on a regular basis, they will gain a true understanding of how your company is operating, evolving and growing. A regular flow of announcements trickling in ideally every two weeks will quickly place your company on key media contacts' radar screens. After a while, some media contacts will keep a file on your company.

Identifying News to Release: I have lost count of the number of times business owners have told me they have no news to announce. Yet after five minutes of brainstorming, an extensive list is developed, and it soon becomes a matter of prioritizing and strategizing which ones to release for the best coverage result. Here are some ideas:

The CRISP Principle study found that 74 percent of high-growth companies regularly received mention in the media. Of these companies, 95 percent sent news releases on a regular basis as part of their marketing program.

- New contracts or clients
- New offerings
- Volunteer or charitable activities
- Professional affiliation involvements or contributions
- Certifications, designations or licenses
- Conferences attended
- Newly launched website
- Expanded market area or market segment
- New or expanded location
- Staff additions, promotions or achievements
- Anniversaries of your business or employees
- Awards or recognitions received from another entity
- Strategic alliances or business affiliations

As you went through this list, you probably thought of numerous announcements you can make about your business. By breaking them down so that each one is a news item, it will help you keep in regular contact with the media with a regular flow of news.

Lasting First Impression

A family-owned training and development company sent out news releases like clockwork every two to three weeks announcing everything from client relationships, completed projects, and staff accomplishments to expanded market areas and new affiliate associates. After about nine months, a reporter with a business newspaper decided to write a story on the company and contacted the owners for an interview. He was surprised to learn the firm's core team was made up of only six members. The reporter had envisioned a much larger company because of the numerous releases he had received. The impression proved to be a valuable one as the final article emphasized how effective a small business could be in serving larger business clientele through effectively leveraging strategic relationships.

Preparing a News Release: A news release should be printed on your company letterhead or placed within the text of an e-mail in a professional manner. At the very top of the release in all capital letters, put FOR IMMEDIATE RELEASE. The next item to appear should be the name of the contact person, along with a phone number and e-mail address. Make the main topic of your release the headline. Keep your releases focused simply on the facts. Write it to answer the who, what, where, why and how. Notice I did not include when? A mistake many people make when sending a release is putting a date on it. Most news being released is not dated unless it is announcing a specific event or date to the media. Otherwise, do not put a date on your release. By not dating the release, you are exponentially increasing your chances of it getting published. When a reporter or editor is going through releases, they discard anything with a date beyond a certain timeframe of their choosing. If your release does not have a date, it will remain in the queue for inclusion.

About six months after my business had moved into a new office, a client called my office jokingly asking if I had moved again. He knew my philosophy about putting dates on releases and was impressed that after several months my move was still getting press. The announcement he was referring to had appeared in a monthly business publication. Typically, a monthly publication is working three to four months ahead of publication. Therefore, had the release about my move been dated, it would have been discarded and not included in the next available issue. The release also noted that the relocation included an expansion of office space, which also was deemed good news to share about a growing company.

The Importance of a Company Profile Paragraph: Every release should include a paragraph about your company. This is a brief overview to remind media contacts what your company does. In addition, you may also be delighted when a small staff-starved publication runs your entire release and includes that paragraph. Information to include are your company's mission, target market, geographical focus, capabilities and products offered, year established and any special recognitions. I also recommend including your website for more information in this paragraph.

The Importance of a Personal Bio Paragraph: Create a biographical paragraph about yourself to include in any release announcing something about you in association with the business. This paragraph should include your title, years in your business or industry, special designations or educational background, specialized areas of expertise, honors and recognitions. This paragraph should only be used when announcing something specifically about you. If the release is about the business, and you are merely being quoted as a spokesperson, do not include it.

Snail Mail vs. E-mail Distribution: With local, regional and trade media, I recommend sending news releases the old- fashioned way – by snail mail. Why? Because the minute you send the release via e-mail, you have dated it. And as I mentioned earlier in this chapter, most news you have to share does not need to be associated with a specific release date. Second, if you have not established a relationship with a media contact, chances are you will be classified as spam or be blocked. Just think about how many e-mails you get and consider how many more a media contact receives.

If you have not established a relationship, you cannot expect an e-mailed release to mean anything to the contact. However, strange as it sounds, it will be noticed if it is mailed. To assure it is recognized as a news release, make certain that on the outside of the envelope below the mailing address you put FOR IMMEDIATE RELEASE and then state the headline of the release. This will distinguish it from other mail and junk mail. If it is identified as a news release, it will be opened and viewed by the recipient. There is one exception to e-mailing releases, and this is to the web editors of various publications. With most media outlets having an online presence, many have designated a web editor to post news on the online version of the publication.

When you grow to a national level in distributing your news to the media, use a combination of e-mail, mail and phone follow-up all at the same time. Because of the massive amount of news a national outlet receives, you want to feed them news in a variety of ways. This includes news distribution wires. For the small business, I recommend free ones such as www.prlog.org and www.i-newswire.com.

Using Photos with Releases: Most releases will not include a photo. But including one when appropriate can double the likelihood your announcement will be used. It can also increase the probability the release will be run as an article in a small suburban publication where your company is located or where you or a staff member live. Make sure it makes sense to include a photo. Don't use photos if they are not relevant to the release. When announcing something about you or an employee, include a head shot with the release. Use a professional photographer for yours. For employees or individuals included in announcements on a limited basis, a passport photo taken at an area commercial photo service can be inexpensively produced. A 3"x5" size is more than sufficient. If you anticipate making regular announcements involving specific individuals, invest in a professional head shot of them. When submitting the photo, type the person's full name on a label attached to the photo, and also note to KEEP ON FILE. This alerts the media you will be sending more releases about this individual so they will archive the photo once they have scanned it.

If you have made a donation to a charity or provided support to a group and have made a special presentation, include a photograph with the announcement. Be sure to write a caption that identifies everyone in the photo on a label you place on the back of photo.

Another way to handle a photograph with a release is to state "Photo (or photos) available upon request electronically" on a separate line at the bottom of the release. The actual hard-copy photo included with the release is best. Sending a CD is not recommended unless you have an entire series of photos. In this case, you would still want a printed reference of the photos included with the CD.

Eventually, you will get to a point with the media on a local level where you will be sending your news electronically and they will be expecting them. Until an editor or reporter requests your news electronically, keep sending the news releases by mail.

Power of the Blurbs: Most of your news releases will be placed in the people on the move, business notes or briefs sections. Don't underestimate the power of these "blurbs." Over a period of six to nine months, this should be your primary expectation. Your initial releases are reinforcing ongoing activity within your company while you are still in an introductory mode with the media. The media commonly sees companies sending out information sporadically, but one that shows true dedication and commitment to getting news out regularly will get noticed. Over time, these announcements will be valuable in establishing top-of-mind awareness among media contacts. This cannot be emphasized enough. It is unrealistic to expect immediate feature coverage or to be contacted as an expert resource after only a handful of releases.

Making it More Newsworthy: Once you get into the habit of sending general announcement releases, you can begin to send some releases that are more news-oriented to create even more interest in your company. The key to doing this effectively is to understand the type of news different media outlets cover. News to one reporter may mean nothing to another because of differing specialized areas of focus. In Secret # 43, I cover this subject by discussing news distribution. There are several things you can do to make a general announcement into a more newsworthy one. Consider why you are announcing a particular news item. What made you decide to add a product, increase your staff or change your company name? If it can be tied into something occurring in the marketplace, you may gain better coverage of the release and more placements.

For instance, a cultural diversity and language training company went through an extensive planning process that resulted in a strategic shift and name change. When one of the owners first drafted the release, she composed a well-written release with an appropriate news tie-in, but missed the mark with a headline that simply stated the company had changed its name. Fortunately, the owner had a marketing professional review the release before sending it. There was only one suggestion: Change the headline to "An ever-growing global marketplace results in company's strategic shift and name change." Within a few weeks, the release appeared in an international business column, business notes and briefs, trade and chamber publications among a myriad of others. Had the release remained with the previous headline, it would have been in about half of these places.

Batteries Never Included

In a world of whiz-bang commercialized toys, an inspired parent was determined to create a different kind of toy store where the imagination and curiosity of the young developing mind were foremost when parents were choosing products. The only thing electronic about this store was its online presence as it touted toys and products with no batteries, blinking lights or cartoon tie-ins. Only educational, motivational and naturally-produced children's toys were offered. Based on a belief there were many other like-minded parents looking for these kinds of toys, the store's mission was as much about bringing the unique to market as it was about bringing old world and traditional child-parent toys back into vogue. Armed with an arsenal of exclusive finds, the company's founders knew that pursuing publicity in key media would not only create awareness, but also credibility with these parents. Through e-mails and hard copy releases about the unique toys being sold, combined with newsworthy points of interest, the media embraced the toy store. With features on everything from items not being made in China and eco-friendly products to toys that were unique and natural or produced in direct support of charities, the company gained local, regional,

national and international exposure in just a few short
months. Every parenting magazine as well as countless
specialty consumer publications and online sources have
featured the company, its products or philosophies. Since
being established in 2004, the store has expanded to
include child gear and furniture as well as toys and was
named among the Inc. 500 with triple-digit growth.

• • •

A well-executed media relations program is the perfect complement to your other marketing efforts. However, don't expect publicity to be your only source of promotion. As with all other marketing tactics, media relations work best as a part of a comprehensive program.

39

Expert Resource

Once your business is viewed as possessing specialized expertise, it can go to levels you only imagined were possible. Growth companies masterfully orchestrate this by identifying, nurturing and fostering opportunities to be positioned and sought after as an expert resource.

Media Resource: If part of your overall strategy is for you or your staff to be perceived as industry or subject-matter experts, your news releases should continually present the expertise when information is released. This makes the bio paragraph mentioned in Secret # 38 even more important. Scrutinize it carefully to make sure it positions you as a knowledgeable expert. In addition, any staff members being positioned as media resources should have one-page bios on your website that include detailed information regarding their areas of expertise. When a reporter or producer is seeking a resource, it is often not during usual business hours. Being able to go to your company website will enable the media contact to confirm you have the expertise they are seeking. They can then reach your company to arrange an interview or have you answer questions via e-mail to make it easier for a reporter on deadline. Being responsive to the media is critical. Calls or e-mails from media contacts should be returned immediately. I also recommend following up any interview – conducted over the phone or in–person – with a note confirming what was discussed. The media person will be appreciative of getting the added insight especially if there is any concern about technical or factual information. Most errors in print articles are not due to any malice. It is simply a writer trying to translate notes on deadline and misinterpreting them in the process.

White Papers & Studies: A white paper is an authoritative report or guide that usually addresses a particular issue or problem and how it can be solved. Publishing white papers or research studies in your marketplace or trade industry is a highly effective means of elevating you, your company or staffer into being recognized as an expert source. Many national industry conferences call for white papers and presentations with the expectation that the information will be released for the first time at the conference. Conducting research and then releasing the results of the study is also an effective means of positioning your company. With the research, you can cite trends, patterns, or a consensus of thinking on a specific matter or area of concentration within your industry or the markets you serve. There is endless value in providing the marketplace with information no one else is providing by conducting unique research or a market analysis. When I completed my analysis of the CRISP Principle study in 2004, I sent a news release that included a handful of the results. I was then asked to present the findings at a Chamber of Commerce Small Business Council meeting. Later, I incorporated the findings into numerous small business classes I was teaching – and now into this book.

Marketing Intelligence

The CEO and co-founder of a regional staffing firm knew that when competition is stiff, you need to differentiate yourself so the marketplace doesn't even consider your competition. She realized the true power of this philosophy when, despite the recession, her firm continued on its fast-growth course while others struggled and downsized. Her strategy was to focus on areas where competitors were not paying attention, then becoming viewed as an expert in these areas. The distinction was that her company focused on trends-based expertise rather than industry-based. The first area of focus was on hiring to create a diverse work environment. Research showed that companies with high retention rates were six times more likely to have a diverse workforce. The CEO was so impassioned by the need for education, resources and understanding in this arena that she founded a nonprofit forum to focus entirely on this purpose. The key to its successful launch and buy-in was the fact it addressed diversity on numerous fronts, not just differences in ethnic cultures. It also covered multi-generational thinking styles and gender differences. Her staffing firm, along with other

> **Being an expert resource to media attracts speaking opportunities. In our research, every business owner or staff member asked to be a resource to the media on issues in business or their industry was also asked to speak as an expert to address groups and organizations.**

corporate partners, funded the nonprofit to provide free or low-cost education to companies that would otherwise not be able to resource the expertise. Very quickly her staffing firm became the go-to firm for companies seeking a diverse workforce. Another area of focus was that while companies hired on skills, they typically fired due to a mismatch between the individual and the corporate culture. Candidates were not being qualified by considering their emotional intelligence (EQ), which would gauge their fit into the company culture. It was evident that having a match with the mentality of the candidate was just as important a success factor as the candidate's skill set. Therefore, the company teamed up with an EQ expert to develop an assessment tool and process. This led to the formation of a separate division that specifically focused on this topic. In addition to white papers and publicity generated from the unique expertise her company brought to the market, there is no greater credibility factor than being recognized as a company that truly practices what it preaches. In 2008 and 2009, the staffing firm was named a Best Place to Work by its employees, underscoring how effective this company is at what it does in the marketplace. With a 40 percent growth rate in 2009 and 20 new clients, the company is on track for more significant growth moving forward. Its co-founders are regularly asked to be a resource to the media, and the company has received numerous recognitions. It was named to its local market's Fast 50 and was named an Inc. 5000 growth company on a national level.

Speaking Resource: An ideal way to present your expertise is to speak to groups and organizations. Many business owners have actually pursued this avenue before embarking on a media relations program. This certainly can work effectively. Just note that someone who is resourced in the news is in greater demand as a speaker. However, if done properly presenting yourself or someone in your company as a speaker can be an excellent means of gaining targeted exposure for your company. Targeting an organization for potential speaking opportunities is no different than targeting an organization for a strategic involvement. The same three criteria mentioned in Secret # 31 apply. When asked to speak as an expert, it is important to be one and leave your sales hat at the door. You have been invited to bring information, insight and knowledge, not to peddle your wares. The reality is that if you show what you know, the business opportunities will come. We have all been in a presentation where we felt jilted because we were being "pitched to" instead of being given nuggets of wisdom. The key is to leave them wanting more rather than heading for the door. Groups will often offer you the opportunity to make promotional material available before and after you speak. Take advantage of it. If you can, have someone staff the "sales" table so you can remain in the "expert" role. But if you are a one-man or one-woman show, just be cognizant of each role and when it is appropriate. Does the idea of speaking in front of a group make you uncomfortable? Then opt to be part of a panel of experts. This can alleviate some pressure and can also help you gain confidence when speaking in front of a crowd.

By-lined Article: As you begin to establish yourself as an expert, opportunities may arise to submit articles to the media. Known as a by-lined article, it is written by you as a contributing writer rather than by someone on staff or a freelance writer. You are writing it from an expert's point of view. A residential designer was sending out releases regularly to local, regional and trade media and some select design and building magazines to keep them informed. Over six months, she had not seen anything published in the trade publications. But then she sent a release that highlighted her being featured in a new product video for a nationally known brand. It caught the attention of one of the magazine editors, who asked her to write a by-lined article on home design trends in her geographic area. See what I mean about calling news releases "love letters to the media?" After six months of sending releases as an FYI, she was published in a trade magazine for the first time as a featured expert. This is the power of media relations.

Guest or Regular Columnist: Small business and community newspapers and magazines are always seeking experts to write on everything from business and technology to gardening and parenting. If you enjoy writing, look through some of your local publications to see if there is a void in subject matter that you could address with a regular column. While the writing would not be for pay in most cases, it offers value to the publication's readership and could later become a paying gig if you decide to syndicate should you grow a readership. Other publications have a column where different contributors provide content. Study these opportunities as well.

Special Interest Blogs: Without a doubt, blogs are no longer something done by someone with too much time on their hands. Blogs are a powerful tool for business. If you can create a blog that focuses on a specific topic, interest or subject matter, all the better. However, it can be time-consuming, so be sure to have a strategy and a planned frequency. If you start out strong and then fade away, it can be more damaging than simply posting when you have something worth posting. You can also designate guest bloggers so the pressure is not all on you.

• • •

In whatever business or industry you are in, you have expertise to share. Consider how you can take what you know and turn it into a true demonstration of your knowledge and skills so you become an expert resource. Growth-oriented business owners have been doing this for decades and enjoying the rewards of being sought out while competitors are being bought out or shut out.

40

Events with a Cause

It is increasingly difficult for businesses to attract attendees when they host events. Just having an open house or customer appreciation event does not hold the same appeal it used to. High-growth businesses understand that their customers' time is valuable. Therefore, to make their events worthwhile, they are tied to a cause or special interest that speaks to customers and makes them want to participate.

Fundraiser Events: One of the best ways to make a client appreciation, open house or anniversary celebration more meaningful is to tie it to raising money for a good cause. Get a little creative, and it becomes an event people will anticipate. You can put the fun into fundraising in a multitude of ways. By the time my business was 15 years old, I was determined to wait until my company turned 21 to throw one heck of a party Why? Because everyone holds 10, 15, 20 and 25-year celebratory events, I was determined to do something different. I had not seen anyone celebrate 21 years in business. When the time came near, we had a blast planning it and even more fun promoting it and doing it. We were able to have it fall on the 21st of the month. A 21-reasons-to-attend campaign created excitement and anticipation weeks ahead of the event. Then the event itself played off the number 21 in as many ways as we could come up with – from carding people as they walked through the door to playing black jack in the back room. At 10:59 p.m., everyone received a lottery ticket as we watched on the TV screen for the winning lottery numbers. No one won, but the anticipation was priceless. We had a 21-gun salute outside in front of the office building featuring everything from a glue gun to a nail gun pointed to the sky. We also conducted a Bazooka Gum salute with 21 people blowing the biggest bubbles known to mankind in unison. For the fundraiser aspect, we asked everyone to donate in an increment of 21. Some people donated $210, others donated $21.21. We raised money for Relay for Life and had a night to remember as well.

Can Can Do

The invitations for a construction company's 30th-anniversary party asked attendees to bring aluminum

cans to the event. For every can received, the company
donated a dollar per can plus matched the overall amount
raised to a local battered women's shelter. How did they
decide on the can angle? Research uncovered that in
1975, the year the company was founded the pull tab now
found on aluminum cans was patented. Recycling and
using resources wisely was a value shared by customers
and the construction firm, so it was a natural tie-in. A
walk down memory lane showed three decades of building
trends and hairstyles. More than 70 people attended the
event, a truckload of cans were recycled, and money was
raised for a worthy charity.

Collection Events: Many businesses find that an annual drive to collect items for the needy is a worthwhile event. It brings people together while also doing good. From collecting toys, school supplies, winter coats and clothing to human hair and items for a community service flea market, there are numerous ways your business can make a collections event a success. There are two ways to approach it. One way is to have an event where everyone brings their donated items. Another approach is to collect items during a designated time period and then make an event out of delivering the goods to the charity.

> *High-growth companies were more likely in the CRISP Principle study to tie a special event to a cause than no-growth companies. Events supporting a cause are viewed as worthwhile and credible. When times are tough, anything viewed as frivolous is also viewed as irresponsible.*

Awareness Events: Some businesses choose to host an event that raises funds and awareness at the same time. It can be related to healthcare, safety or an industry. There is a great website, www.brownielocks.com, which lists every imaginable awareness day, week, and month known in the world. It is a great way to generate ideas for tie-ins for anything from events to news.

Cause & Effect

An events business had become the go-to company for
unique high-profile events throughout the region, which
was a center for the banking industry. When the
recession hit, budgets were cut dramatically and lavish

*events were considered inappropriate. With national
headlines blasting financial institutions for irresponsible
behavior that caused the recession and for allegedly using
TARP monies for bonuses and six-figure events, it
appeared the event planning industry was dead. But not
for this forward-thinking and hands-on entrepreneur
and her team, who had been through two other down
economies. What made her events company unique was
that the owner understood that events were a branding
opportunity. When done properly, they could have long-
term effects that went far beyond the event itself. In
addition, the firm had established strong connections
with multiple market sectors, including industry,
corporate, government, charitable and educational. With
these extensive contacts, they kept a pulse on the
marketplace and so were poised and ready to shift as
needed. While lavish events were out, charitable and
cause-focused events were in. Because of the company's
wide scope of reach and because it was considered the best
in its industry, it was the preferred provider of these
events. Moreover, it was not just involved in the
execution, but also in the actual creation of what the
event would be and ultimately achieve. Her company had
effectively elevated its stature as more than an events
company. It was also a strategic partner focused on
events that made a difference. Best of all for this
entrepreneur, her hopes to build a company that would
live and thrive beyond her was realized. At age 50, she
sold her business and was able to totally focus on making
a difference in truly personal and profound ways.*

• • •

Considering Secrets #33, #34, and now #40, the message is clear — giving
back is the way growth companies conduct business. The old adage that "the
more you give, the more you get" certainly rings true for these companies. It
can for you, too.

41

Leadership Roles

A business owner must wear many hats within his or her business. But savvy owners also understand the value of taking on leadership roles beyond their companies to build a solid business presence within the marketplace. They know that a leadership role – especially when done well – draws powerful public awareness that can attract a wide circle of influential followers and admirers ready and willing to assist. These roles include being an ambassador, an advocate, and an industry or thought leader. Which one works best for you depends on your passions and interests.

In Secret #31, we discussed the reasons to be involved in groups and the criteria for selecting ones to help drive business growth. In this secret, we will discuss this in more depth. Specifically, we'll look at the different leadership roles you can embrace that will elevate your stature in the marketplace while also elevating the presence of your business.

The Ambassador: Being an ambassador is being a leader who continually helps others make connections while representing a common interest or group. This can include serving in a government cabinet or advisory council, chairing a chamber welcoming committee, or heading up an economic development site visitation committee. Some groups have a community outreach or board liaison position whose sole purpose is to represent the group at other organizations' functions. These roles place you in front of high-level influencers who can enhance your connections.

The Advocate: Being an advocate is being an activist. You lead efforts to effect change or protect the interests of a group or cause. You help a group take a stand. In some cases, it can lead to other public relations opportunities. For example, as part of my advocacy efforts related to unfair small business tax legislation, I was asked to speak at a press conference in Boston in 2004 in association with the National Restaurant Association and the National Association of Women Business Owners. The press conference called for restoring the business meal tax deduction to 100 percent from the reduced amount of 50 percent. It received national news coverage and brought awareness to an issue affecting small business. In another instance, I chaired a national procurement task force of business owners that reviewed federal government contracting practices with small businesses. The end result was a white paper that identified 11 critical challenges with 34 recommendations for government agencies to take to overcome or address the challenges. As chair, I presented the findings at a national public policy conference. Other taskforce members presented the findings and recommendations before legislative committees and agencies.

When considering an advocacy leadership role, keep in mind there will likely be controversy. You need to be comfortable with taking the heat as much as leading the group to glory.

Families First

A family law attorney envisioned a practice that made family values and children's best interests a top priority. This belief was at the core of how she practiced law and how she worked with and helped divorcing clients. Even before she started her own firm, she immersed herself in all aspects of the family law community and became an advocate for children. By doing this, she was able to understand and continually focus on the best solutions for her clients in the court system. She became involved in a variety of ways: serving on the domestic court bar committee and women's bar association, participating in business leader groups and becoming a nationally certified literacy tutor. She also led charitable efforts that sponsored needy families during the holidays. In 2008, she struck out on her own to form a different kind of law firm and was amazed at the peer support she received. After more than a decade of practicing what she preached, she had gained immense respect from peers, judges and the community at large. With her new practice, she continued all she had been doing, taking it to a higher level of involvement within

In our CRISP Principle study, more than 80 percent of high-growth business owners served on leadership boards of at least one or two organizations. More than half of them had served on the executive level as president or chair of an organization.

the community. She hosted family law events at her new office, took on a pro bono case each month and conducted free educational events for families and peers. More than 76 percent of her new clients referrals come from judges, peers and clients. Her firm is considered the first choice for domestic cases involving any issues related to separation, divorce, custody, alimony, property division and domestic violence. Within 18 months of opening her firm, it had grown to five attorneys in two offices. It was named one of the Top 50 entrepreneurial firms in its market area, proving that putting families first was not only good for children, but was also a first-rate plan for growth.

The Industry Leader: An industry leader takes a leadership role within his or her professional trade industry. If your goal is to become an expert in your industry, this can be a powerful launching pad. The assumption is that if you are a respected leader within your industry, you must be good at what you do. Opportunities exist at local, state, national and international levels. An insulation supplier business owner and his team became active with green building and sustainability initiatives within the local home builders association. Then they got involved regionally and nationally by forming a buying consortium focused on green products, best practices and policies. As a result, they were honored with an award from a local business publication for being a green building advocate and leader.

The Community Leader: Stepping up to be a community leader can encompass anything from being chairman of the local chamber of commerce to leading a United Way or community-oriented event. It can also be an appointment by a government official to lead a special project or effort. If you are interested in getting involved in any of these types of groups, the local chamber of commerce is a good starting point for information.

Curtain Call

A marketing and public relations firm owner enjoyed attending performances of the local community theater. In addition, the group's drama camp was an excellent activity for her children during the summer. After performances were cancelled due to lack of funds, she joined the board to see how she could contribute in rebuilding the group. She quickly stepped into the role of president, focusing on revitalizing the organization through a diverse board of needed expertise. Her firm adopted the theater group as a pro bono commitment, becoming a sponsor and producing all its promotional materials and performance playbills. She served as a spokesperson for the group and as a community liaison with other arts groups to foster collaboration. She nurtured her media contacts to build awareness and support from the community. Three years later, because of those efforts, the group was back producing four productions a year in addition to operating its successful drama camp. By leading efforts to help save a valued community group, this business owner continues to realize opportunities for her business because of the connections and difference she made.

The Thought Leader: The opinion and editorial pages are the most popular section of the newspapers read by community movers, shakers and government officials. Writing a guest editorial or a letter to the editor can make a powerful impression on those with influence and has the power to elevate your image in the community. However, a word of caution is warranted. Make sure your facts are correct and that they support your opinion. Be careful not to appear to be ranting or let your emotions outweigh the logical points you are making. There is no guarantee your piece will be published. However, if it does get published it can bring attention to you as a business owner willing to take a stand.

Another option is to contact an editor or reporter to propose the publication do a feature story on a particular topic based on your perspective. Encourage them to gain insights on the subject from others. This is a perfect opportunity for you to position yourself as a resource.

After I moved my company and home to their current locations, I learned there was a planned highway expansion that would take away a portion of my neighborhood. Further investigation revealed the Department of Transportation was considering alternative routes that would relocate fewer businesses and impact fewer homes. As a result of this knowledge, community associations joined forces to form a citizens group to create awareness and support for these alternatives. I contacted the media encouraging them to attend the public hearing and I was interviewed by local media outlets. The power of the people prevailed and one of the alternative routes was chosen.

Blogging has also become a popular way to become a thought leader across the Internet. Once a following goes viral, the ability to leverage it can be powerful and sometimes take on a life of its own, with your blog posts being reposted on other sites.

●   ●   ●

When considering any leadership role, be aware that it will undoubtedly be time-consuming. When you commit to it, be clear about what it will entail to ensure you can fulfill the responsibilities. One of the most damaging things you can do for your image and that of your company is to make a commitment and then drop the ball. This holds true for your employees as well. If they take a leadership role as a representative of your company, truly support them in their efforts. The reality is that unfulfilled or broken promises are remembered much longer than ones that are kept.

42

Award Winning

If you want to be considered the best in your industry, seeking awards for your business should be a part of your strategy. Award-winning companies are viewed as more credible, stable and worthy of patronizing. If you are in a creative, innovative, or progressive business or want to be viewed as such, being honored for these traits can effectively position you as the best – with the recognition to back it up. Winning awards or being named a finalist also brings extensive media exposure. You can leverage articles or profiles related to the award in your marketing materials and on your website. For some businesses, winning awards becomes a competitive advantage because it makes them unique in their industry. Others are probably not seeking awards, which presents you with powerful opportunities. By being the first to be recognized within your industry, you improve your image in the marketplace.

Many business owners do not realize the number of opportunities that exist for a business to be named "the best" or where to begin to identify them. Google can easily open your eyes to the world of awards. Start your search by keying in "business award" or "service award" and add where you are located. Voila! There's a list of many of the awards given in your local market. Do the same for your industry. Understanding the various type of awards can help you decide how to include this component of public relations into your strategy.

Product & Capability Awards: Depending upon your industry, there can be a plethora of award opportunities. Begin with your professional trade associations. Also look at professional trade magazines and journals. There may be an annual conference or event where awards are presented, and the winners are profiled in a special edition. For example, a neurological medical device company received a best new product award from an occupational therapy magazine, thereby giving the product national exposure and credibility within the medical community. Numerous industries recognize innovation and creativity. The key is to identify award programs that make sense for you to enter. This includes considering the time and potential costs of entering. Some awards charge a fee while others do not.

Entrepreneurial Awards: Being recognized as a well-managed company tells customers you are not only good at what you do, but are also a business that will stand the test of time through solid management and operational practices. Entrepreneurial awards are plentiful at the local, state and national levels. Chambers of commerce and business owner groups often recognize entrepreneurial achievement. The U.S. Small Business Administration recognizes companies in every state in conjunction with its annual Small Business Week.

Winner's Choice

Print publications across the country reduced their page counts in 2009 in response to Corporate America's advertising and marketing budget cuts. At the same time, a regional design firm realized double-digit growth while competitors were struggling. An integral part of this success was the image-building strategy of its owner and founder. After 12 years in business, the firm had built a solid reputation for its work with magazines, catalogs, custom books, newsletters and marketing materials. More than 50 local, regional and national awards attested to its creativity and innovation in design. However, other competitors had also won design awards, so the owner knew it was not enough to differentiate her firm and position it as the firm of choice. She decided her firm would pursue award opportunities that also honored it for being well-managed and progressive. She knew that validating her company's staying power as a well-managed company would further set it apart from competing design firms. Identifying numerous opportunities on the local, regional and national levels, she submitted her firm for consideration for a variety of awards. In 2009, in addition to receiving five design awards, she and her firm were recognized with nine others, including a Top Entrepreneur award, a

> **More than 70 percent of high growth companies in the CRISP Principle study had received awards for products or services. They were also five times more likely to have received recognition with awards for business management or entrepreneurial achievement.**

prestigious college alumni award and a Top 100 North Carolina business award. She was also named one of the Enterprising Women of the Year on a national level. Her firm, however, gained its most coveted recognition when it received an international Stevie® Award for best business turnaround because of her proactive approach in shifting her business model in anticipation of market conditions. Her firm is now a regional design powerhouse serving clients in five states with plans to expand throughout the Southeast. Her appreciation for the prestige and credibility awards bring to a firm gave her solid gold results and an ever-growing client base that knows they are working with the very best.

Company Awards: Whether as a best place to work or for business ethics, there are an array of awards recognizing companies for a particular area in which they excel. An engineering firm was named a finalist for a business ethics award where the other finalists were significantly larger in size and scope. This recognition remains a source of great pride for the firm as it is the only engineering firm in the marketplace to receive the honor so far.

Individual Achievement Awards: You or your employees can also be considered for a variety of awards. Across the country, business newspapers and magazines recognize individual achievements in either a listing or a single award. Trade industries recognize member service within an organization, and even universities recognize alumni making their mark in the business world.

Offering Awards & Recognition: Another way to leverage awards is by giving them to others. Examples include scholarship awards, supplier awards, employee awards, distributor or dealer awards. The owner of a computer networking and hardware installation company was thrilled to be a finalist for a well-known award that recognized fast growth. In response, the firm decided to give special recognition plaques to each customer that year as a way of saying thanks. The gesture evolved into an annual recognition with one customer being named a pinnacle partner of excellence.

Take some time to investigate the opportunities that exist within your local marketplace and trade industry first. See what is entailed in time and potential costs and make submitting for awards a part of your marketing program if you see some opportunities that can help support your strategic positioning and awareness goals.

To follow are some do's and don'ts to get you started on the path to award-winning success.

DO have a Web presence. In the CRISP Principle study, we found a direct correlation between those who won multiple awards or recognitions and those with a website. Companies with a website were five times more likely to have won a management or entrepreneurial award. Now, this is not to say having a website will win you an award. Other factors also play into it. However, within a month after discovering this correlation in the research, I was among a judging panel for an Entrepreneur of the Year awards program. We were charged with narrowing a semi-finalist field from six to three candidates. One of the six businesses did not have a website. It received the lowest score at this level of the qualifying because the judging panel all agreed that in spite of being a leader in many aspects, it did not make sense with everything else the business was doing that it did not have a web presence.

DON'T view it as win or lose. Yes, it's a competition. But it is also a marketing opportunity. By remembering this, you will get a lot more mileage out of the recognition. Numerous awards name finalists to create excitement and increase attendance to an event that names the winner. In these cases, the publicity is most aggressive before the event. The impact this can have on exposure for your business is significant. In 1998, 2000 and 2006, my company was named a finalist in a local entrepreneur of the year awards program. We never did win, yet people remember we had been named a finalist several times. These same people often can't remember who actually won, yet they remember my company being a finalist. That demonstrates how leveraging a recognition at any level is the key to creating maximum exposure for your company.

DO have a professional head shot. When you are pursuing this level of recognition, you are expected to have a professional head shot. Most entities will ask for one if you are named a finalist or a winner for use in their materials about the award. Don't take a snapshot with your digital camera no matter how tempting that may seem. When the photo is published, it will stand out as one of lesser quality, making you look less polished and professional compared to others.

DON'T always rely on the entity to publicize. While many organizations will send a news release about the honor, others only communicate within their own community. You will get better coverage if you release the information on your own – especially if you send it to smaller and suburban media. In addition your neighborhood or industry trade publications like to receive news of this nature and will most likely publish the announcement along with your photo.

DON'T just focus on awards in your specific industry. Seek out awards that also demonstrate your community service, entrepreneurship, management savvy or unique approach to a certain aspect of your business. A residential designer had won countless local, national and regional awards for her home designs. However, her competitors had won similar awards. Seeing an opportunity to set her company apart, she pursued awards for management practices. Winning them gave her firm additional credibility.

DO create a nomination network. In many cases, a nomination must be submitted by another person or entity. Make your interest in a particular award known among those you think would be willing to nominate you. Also collect testimonials and letters of recommendation that can be used as documentation when submitting award nominations. Reference letters are often requested as a part of the application process and should be personalized to the awarding entity's judging panel.

•   •   •

Whether the award is from your local chamber of commerce, a professional trade association or a business publications, pursuing them – and then receiving them – can open doors of opportunities that would have been closed otherwise.

43

Power of the Press

Evolving from news provider to information insider can propel your stature and your business to levels that you only dreamed of when you initially launched a media relations campaign in your business. Once the media sees that your business is a flow of ongoing news and information, you will find that they will seek you out for possible ideas and opportunities versus you always being the one to take the initiative.

Those who gain this level of exposure and respect have earned it. How? By respecting the media and what they are trying to do. One of the biggest mistakes I see business owners make is to call the media right out of the gate without any releases or communications whatsoever to back them up. The call is to tell the reporter or editor about his or her exciting new business. While the passion and enthusiasm is commendable, it is not a story, it is not news, and it is not of interest to the media contact. Anything you offer must either provide news or information that would be deemed of value to the readership, listenership, or viewership.

Local & Regional Print Media: No one has been hit harder by the economy and the public's migration to the Internet than the print media. Newspapers and magazines across the country have made significant staff cutbacks. The size of their issues has shrink as a result of fewer advertisers and fewer readers. The smart publications have jumped to the Internet with an online presence to support and enhance their print version. Because of staff cuts, news and information that can easily be regurgitated on their pages is highly valued. Remaining staff members want to be viewed as bringing value to the publication to avoid being the next one laid off. Feeding them news and information they can easily turn into a story or brief helps them do their job better. The secret to gaining coverage in the print media is to send your news and information to specific multiple contacts on a regular basis. Send your releases to the editor, managing editor, associate editor, small business reporter, regional reporter and any editors or reporters that specialize in your industry. You will send to several people at one publication, but that is okay as each is charged with putting news in the publication in a different way. One news release from a business owner generated three separate placements at the same daily publication over the course of a week as a result of three different media contacts picking up tidbits relevant to their focus areas. The release was about an event being conducted in association with a restaurant to raise money for a charity. The release appeared different days of the week in the food notes section in the main paper, the business notes section in a suburban section, and in a section that shared news about community philanthropy efforts.

Another mistake business owners make is to disregard the power of the local press when their company is national in scope and conducts most of its business outside of their base of operations. If your business is national or international, you should still be sending releases to your local marketplace. Local media especially want to hear about local companies doing well on a national or international level. As stated earlier, many of these local publications have an online presence. News about you that's posted on their online edition will be found by those using search engines to find out about your services, products or a specific piece of information about your industry or specialty on a national level. Numerous times I have seen a local story catch the attention of the Associated Press or a regional or national media outlet, who then decides to do a story on the business for national distribution.

Local TV & Radio: Many businesses only send news to the print media because it is assumed television and radio will not be interested. While it is harder to obtain coverage from these mediums because of the immediacy of the news they report, there are, however, immense opportunities. When dealing with TV and radio stations, you need to understand the difference between hard and soft news. Hard news is late-breaking, hot topic, here today, gone tomorrow types of news. Soft news is news that can be shared at any time, which places it in the "filler" category. Most news you share about your business will be soft news easily put on the back burner. If you understand when soft news information is sought and valued and also provide information and insights relevant to hard news stories, you can increase your chances of getting coverage.

> *Growth companies understand that public relations is the most powerful business builder a company has within its control when done the right way. The power of the press in combination with the Internet is easily documented when you begin to receive daily alerts in your email inbox.*

On the hard news side, pay attention to what is the current news focus and figure out how your business can contribute a unique perspective on the subject. With government spending being an ongoing topic on the national front, a local manufacturer was able to leverage a positive story on how they were helping a local government agency significantly reduce spending with recycling and green initiatives. A local news channel picked up the story and ran it numerous times.

Many local TV stations offer news programs during weekend mornings when they are more likely to cover softer news items. The key is to understand the types of feel-good or information-based stories these segments highlight, so you can propose an idea of true value to their viewership. There are also locally-produced TV programs where you can be a guest for commentary and insight. A half-hour TV program focusing on philanthropy within the community invited me for a ten-minute interview to discuss my research findings on small businesses' community involvement and charitable giving. You may also find opportunities to be a regular guest on a TV or radio program. After learning about the audience, you may be able to propose a segment offering tips and information they will value and appreciate.

Star Student

While it seemed anyone serving the residential and commercial construction market had taken a significant hit in 2008, you would have never known it from looking at one interior design professional who experienced double-digit growth. Seeing how the market had shifted and how it negatively impacted her peers, she knew she could not take growth for granted as she prepared to take her firm national. Realizing she was not incorporating public relations into her solid mix of marketing initiatives, she attended a half-day workshop in December 2008 on how to put muscle into a marketing program using public relations. Armed with knowledge gleaned from the workshop, she immediately put what she had learned into action. Her news releases went out like clockwork every two weeks sharing details of her company's growth, offerings, expansions, design and decorating tips and projects. Focusing first on the immediate market area where she was based, she and others, soon saw announcements in area papers. She then contacted the media to offer her expertise as a designer to help consumers achieve "wow-inspiring" decorating on a tight budget. By March 2009, she had gained feature coverage in all of the major local business and consumer media and was doing a regular guest appearance as a "design diva" on a morning radio show. Within six months she was a regular guest columnist for several print publications, including a home and living magazine, a city magazine and a suburban weekly newspaper. This caught the attention of a nationally-renowned organizer of home, holiday and women's expositions that drew thousands of consumers during weekend runs. The organizer made this PR-savvy entrepreneur the exclusive interior designer presenting seminars at her events covering topics such as holiday décor, outdoor decorating and creating beautiful interiors on a budget. Ending 2009 with a record 260 percent growth over 2008, the designer confirms that if you take what you learn to heart, you will reap far beyond what could have expected otherwise. She has started the new decade with a national presence as a contributor to AOL.com and BlogTalkRadio with numerous national exposure opportunities continuing to flow in along with a growing number of clients.

Trade Media: Supplying information to professional trade media can be an excellent way to position your company as one with best practices within your industry. You can share a case study in unison with a client, prepare information about upcoming trends and how you are responding to them, or release the findings of useful research you have conducted. You can then leverage this coverage with local media, which loves to share how an area company is gaining national attention. Therefore, once you receive national industry coverage, send a release to local media announcing the exposure. Many trade association journals and newsletters offer opportunities for members to submit articles for consideration. When you get one published, announce it to your various local media.

Online Media & Using the Internet: Media that strictly appears online is growing by leaps and bounds. From eZines and AOL to BlogTalkRadio, there are limitless opportunities to highlight your business on the Internet. The best part of online media and online content resources is that it is automatically archived and accessible with a click via search engines. Once you or your business appears in an online story or article, you will continue to appear in search engine results as people seek information. Even local television programs are using YouTube to post their segments on the Web for wider reach and exposure. As recommended in Secret #38, submitting your information using free newswire services should be a regular part of your news submittal process. Once it appears through the newswires, the information may be picked up by other Internet sources as well. An article about your company or a by-lined article you have written is often "repurposed" on other online content and news sites. This is when you can truly see the power of the Internet. Within 10 days, an article I wrote as a contributing writer to *Women Entrepreneur* was repurposed on *Entrepreneur, FoxBusiness, AT&T Small Business, Business Insider* and *Yahoo Small Business*. Within 30 days, its exposure had grown to more than 30 different news sources republishing or quoting portions of the article to their audiences.

Google Alerts: As you begin your media relations program, I strongly recommend you submit your company name, product or service names and your name to Google Alerts. They will send you an alert citing the source and the context whenever new references about you appear on the Internet. You can then click on the link to see the coverage in more detail. Yahoo, MSN, AOL and many others also offer this as a free service. As alerts come in, you can then leverage the information for promotional and marketing purposes, such as sharing the links with clients or prospects through e-mail or postings to your social media site.

•   •   •

Including public relations as an integral part of your marketing effort can be a powerful tool for reaching your target markets. The credibility associated with being mentioned in a news story is beyond anything you can achieve with an ad or brochure. The awareness a reader, listener, viewer or Internet user gains about your business or expertise from an unbiased source is priceless. The best part of all is that by doing it strategically – and perhaps with some writing assistance – it can be your most cost-effective tactic offering the biggest return among your core marketing initiatives.

SUPPLEMENTAL
TACTICS

44

Advertising

If you have spent a large part of your budget on advertising and feel your money has been wasted, chances are you're right. Don't get me wrong. Advertising can be highly effective when used as a strategic component of an overall marketing mix. The problem is that for all too many small business start-ups, it is the only component. Both commercial enterprises and consumers have a love-hate relationship with advertising. When you go through a magazine or newspaper, you probably aren't looking for ads. You're looking for content and information or perhaps entertainment.

But think about the ads you do notice. Some catch your eye because of their creative design or messaging. But it's highly unlikely you believe them on face value. You are more likely to be motivated to take action because it was placed in just the right way to be relevant to you at just that moment. Or because it left an impression in conjunction with a myriad of others from friends, family members, colleagues, or related items you have read. In other words, the main reason an ad is often noticed is because of familiarity made possible by a combination of reference points — not just by a single direct appeal or a repeated ad.

If you only use print ads, you will be ignoring many ideal prospects. They may not read print publications or opt to get their news online. With the wide variety of ways people get information, a company cannot afford to put all its marketing dollars into one tactic. It must be strategic to determine if and when advertising will work.

Supplemental vs. Core: Ad placements should not be your primary means of promotion. Rather, it should supplement your core marketing initiatives. In the five previous sections of this book, we discussed several tactics to incorporate into your business in the areas of customer relations, referral relations, Internet presence, strategic involvements and public relations. In Secrets #47 through #50, we will discuss how these five core initiatives can seamlessly work together in strategic ways to accomplish your objectives. You'll need to shift your view about advertising and where and how it is best used. You may find you do not need to advertise at all because your core initiatives are working so well. You can only know for sure by taking a step back and bringing true strategy into play.

When you combine your dollars with good business sense, you will be amazed at how much more effective your advertising will be.

Mission Essential

A leading provider of translators, interpreters and cultural advisors to the military, intelligence agencies and international development organizations realized a strong brand strategy with distinctive marketing and image elements was essential to its growth. To supplement its core marketing initiatives, the company developed a series of trade media ads to educate its primary target audience, differentiate itself from its competitors and increase awareness. The campaign focused on its expertise in providing people for specialized support roles. The first series of four ads boldly proclaimed: "We Don't Build Ships;" "We Don't Design Satellites;" "We Don't Make UAVs" (Unmanned Aerial Vehicles); "We Don't Build Aircraft." A subheading stated "WE KNOW PEOPLE" which was supported by succinct content that explained the company's ability to recruit, train and deploy the most skilled experts in the world. A second ad campaign was designed to complement the first, with a message specifically highlighting the company's services. While competitors promised the world, this company delivered the best people in the world. The powerful headlines read: " EVERY – Everyone. Everywhere. Every Time.; MANY – Many People. Many Places. Many Successes.; NEVER – Never Worry. Never Wonder. Never Fail.; ALWAYS – Always Ready. Always Certain." Combined with emotionally relevant

In the CRISP Principle study, growth companies spent less on advertising than stagnant or no-growth companies and their advertising gained better results. More than 80 percent of growth companies were not using advertising as a primary promotional tactic.

visuals and crisp copy, the ads clearly differentiated the firm from its competitors. The ads were also unlike any seen before in the marketplace, effectively creating cross-market awareness and a preference for the company's language services, intelligence support, training and technical services. Growing from $2.5 million in revenue in 2005 to more than $375 million in 2009, the company solidified its place as a provider of the very best people to international or domestic missions.

Targeted vs. Frequency: Print advertising contracts clearly demonstrate the influence of big business on small business marketing. To gain any special pricing consideration, a 4x, 6x, 13x, 26x or 52x contract must be signed. This means you agree to place an advertisement the contracted number times within a specified time period. You'd think the savings would be substantial, but in most cases they are inconsequential and rarely justify placing more ads than you need. But they are worthwhile for big businesses as their budgets allow for high frequency and the ability to execute multiple tactics on many fronts. Sales reps focused more on their commissions than on your needs will claim you waste money unless you buy frequent exposures in their medium. Yet they never say no when a savvy advertiser chooses to place ads outside of a contract.

Here lies the fallacy of a "frequency" mindset in advertising. Small businesses are typically on a limited budget. In order to have the frequency urged by the sales rep, they place their entire budget in one medium. The unfortunate outcome is money wasted on something that doesn't generate results. The advertising is deemed useless and owners are left frustrated and disenchanted.

If you are heavily focused on ads, stop all of them. Over the next several months implement some of the core tactics we have discussed. After creating an Internet presence in combination with ongoing public relations and strategic involvements, you may consider selectively placing ads in highly-targeted publications. Clients that follow this advice have been surprised when they receive calls from ads appearing less frequently but more strategically. The accumulative exposure gained from the Internet, public relations and strategic involvements led to awareness that give ads more credibility and merit. The targeted audience notices them more. These businesses also re-evaluate the approach and message of their ads, as well as how they determine where to place them.

Strategic vs. Standard Placement: When you decide to advertise in a particular medium, being strategic about how and why you place your ads is critical to your success. There are several aspects to consider when placing an ad.

- <u>Publication Choice</u>: Do not fall prey to thinking that because your competitors advertise in a particular publication, you should, too. Don't be one of many when you can identify alternatives where you are the only one or one of a few. This is another situation where truly understanding your ideal target market and their interests is of vital importance. For instance, a landscape architecture firm advertised in local custom home magazines along with all of its key competitors. In profiling his ideal customers, the owner realized many of them enjoyed the theater and other cultural events. They also enjoyed entertaining outdoors at their homes. The landscape was viewed as an important extension of their entertainment space. Using this insight, the firm became a sponsor of cultural groups, which included advertising in the programs handed out at each event. Focusing on the patrons' love of entertaining and of being entertained, their ads combined the two from an outdoor living space perspective. They were the only landscape architects in the programs, so literally had a captive audience to see their ads and so reaped the rewards of this exclusive exposure.

- Ad Size Choice: Once you have identified the right publications, it's time to strategically choose the ad size to maximize the likelihood it will be noticed. Start by looking at the publication's layout. Some publications group ads together on certain pages. If this is the case, I suggest reconsidering your choice. Think about why a person looks through a publication. They are not looking for ads to read, they are looking for articles to read. So if your ad is not going to appear amidst the publication's articles, it is less likely to be seen. If you see that ads are intermingled with the editorial content, look at the size options for the ads. You want to choose a size that guarantees placement within that content. The best options to choose are a two-thirds page, an island, a one-third page or a vertical half-page. Avoid horizontal half-pages, eighth- or quarter-pages and full-page sizes. A two-thirds page size is not as typical, but is a great alternative to a full page because copy must be used to fill the remaining space. An island-sized ad, which often looks like a horizontal half-page turned vertical, also dominates a page with editorial content on it. A third-page ad also forces the layout to include copy. A half-page vertical ad, while narrow and tall, stands out, too. Although a publication will not hesitate to stack two half-page horizontal ads on a page, they typically only put one vertical half-page ad on a page to allow for copy in the interior portion of the page.

- Positioning Choice: The next thing to consider is where the ad appears within the publication. A right-hand page is the desired placement because people tend to look to the right after turning a page and then linger there before turning to the next one. You should also consider requesting placement in an area with a particular content focus, based on what your ideal market is likely to read. Many publications charge an additional 10 to 15 percent premium for this special position, but it is worth the additional fee. Because you are being more targeted, you are spending more strategically, which will lead to a better return. However, do not hesitate to negotiate waiving the positioning fee under the guise of testing the publication.

Informative & Promotional: Don't just promote your business in your advertising. You should show your ideal market that you understand them better than any of your competitors. Speak to them in a way that makes them stop and think or inspires them to action in some way. A print ad is a visual and verbal image piece. A radio ad is a verbal image piece, although audio in nature. A TV ad is a combination of visual and audio. Never forget that what is seen and heard makes impressions. So be consistent and powerful in what you communicate. Consider what your best value offense is. For businesses that focus on their distinctive expertise, I often recommend an ad that serves as a tips piece or poses a question. I also recommend copy that inspires the reader to either take action or to feel a certain way. If all your ad does is say what you do, you are missing the mark. You need to share what makes you different and what makes you the preferred choice.

To Advertise or Not to Advertise: Small businesses are often convinced the first thing they need to do when they open their doors is advertise. Then they jump into it without really thinking it through. I once met with a new business owner who was frustrated by the lack of success in his marketing efforts. I suggested he use his limited resources to become involved in a strategic group, optimize his Internet presence and begin a public relations program. He looked at me incredulously, saying then he could not afford to advertise — even though he admitted the ads had produced no results! Another business owner was convinced she needed to advertise, but had no idea where. In interviews we conducted with clients across the five key industries she was targeting, we identified more than 30 publications. It was clear her limited budget would not allow her to advertise in all of them. However, public relations proved extremely effective at a fraction of the cost as her firm's news releases were published in many of these same publications. With so many advertising options to choose from, it can be mind-boggling. Here are some basic factors to consider when analyzing advertising as a valid component of your marketing program.

- Print Advertising: As mentioned earlier, just because everyone else is advertising in a particular publication doesn't mean you should, too. Base your decision on what your customers are doing, not what your competitors are doing. Ask your customers what they read on a regular basis and where they notice advertising. Identify more thoroughly your ideal customers' interests. This will enable you to better identify strategic advertising opportunities your competitors have not considered because they are focused on where the industry is advertising rather than on what customers resource.

- Radio Advertising: Radio is most effective when used in conjunction with billboards. You gain a targeted focus of a very specific demographic audience during drive-time periods to and from work. Drive time is the period, typically between 6-10 am and 4-7 pm, when people are commuting back and forth between home and work. You may do a flight schedule of placement over a period of a few weeks, then stop, and start again depending on your budget and planned promotion. The key is knowing if your targeted audience is listening at that time. If your market is not a white collar worker with a 9-5 job, radio may not work for you. You need to understand when your target market is typically listening. If your target reach is a wide age demographic, radio may not be the best choice either. Your budget may not allow you to advertise on all the stations necessary to effectively reach your targeted customers.

- TV Advertising: For TV advertising to be effective, you must understand and verify your target markets' viewing habits. Ask them – don't assume you know. Advertising on cable TV is typically more affordable, and you can generally identify the specific programming your target audience watches on a regular basis. For example, a gymnastics academy successfully used cable TV by targeting children's programming.

- Billboard Advertising: Billboards can be highly effective, but must be carefully scrutinized in large market areas. If your business is located on the outskirts or in the suburbs away from the main thoroughfares, you can obtain billboard space at a significantly reduced rate. A community propane gas company only places billboard advertising in the fall and winter months when purchasing propane for use during the cold is most on users' minds.

• • •

Small businesses simply cannot afford to put all their marketing dollars in one tactical area. Their efforts and financial investments must reap results. Take a look at your core initiatives and what you need to do to improve your efforts in these areas. Then selectively build off of them with supplemental initiatives such as advertising where and when necessary.

45

Direct Mail Done Right

Many business owners never try direct mail because they immediately think "junk mail." You only need to look at the mail you get at work and at home to know that for the most part, there is a great deal of truth in this. Most of the mail people get is junk. However, if done right, direct mail can be a highly effective means of promoting your business and bringing in sales.

Post Cards vs. Mailers: If a piece of mail must be opened for its message to be seen, it decreases the chance it will be read by someone who has not done business with you. Think about your own approach to opening mail. You typically only open mail from businesses or people you know. Therefore, if you do a direct mail campaign where most of your contact list are prospects, an oversized postcard is your best bet. A post card does not require opening. The message is right there for any eyes to see. Even if standing over a trash receptacle while going through the mail, the recipient is going to see what you have to say.

You have a split second to get their attention while they are going through the mail, so get to the point immediately with a post card. An oversized card will stand out among the envelopes. I recommend a size between 5.5 x 8.5 inches up to 6 x 10 inches. You will pay first class postage rather than the post card rate, but the additional cents are worth it. The post card rate is based on a much smaller size which is easily lost or missed in the mail. Businesses also often err in the design of the post card. Again, think about how you go through your mail. The address side is placed up. Therefore, your strongest message needs to be displayed on the same side to get the recipient to turn the card over and read more.

An oversized card gives you "leftover" space to add a message after leaving enough room for the mailing information and the required space the post office requires to process the mail. Use the space located on the left to pose a question or emotionally speak to your target market. Your first objective is to get the recipient to read the piece, then to be inspired to read more and to ultimately keep the piece. If all you have on the address side of the card is the recipient's name and address and your logo, there's only a 25 percent likelihood your card will be read. Give them a reason to turn the card over by appealing to them on a personal level.

Invitations vs. Announcements: When telling people about an event at your location, make it more special by presenting it as an invitation rather than an announcement. While an announcement will suffice on a post card, an invitation is in a sealed envelope with extra touches that make it more personal and more appealing to open. If you can hand address the envelope so it feels like a personal invitation, do so. If no one at your company has good handwriting, use a distinctive typeface – some mimic real handwriting – so it looks special.

Targeted vs. Mass Mailed: Between printing costs and postage, direct mail can be quite costly if you don't have a good handle on who you are targeting. The mailing list is typically where most businesses make poor decisions when deciding to do direct mail. It is often not targeted enough. In direct mail, it is about quality of leads and not their quantity. It is also about segmenting within a larger list to effectively target the message towards the selected segments.

Tail Wagging Welcome

A neighborhood veterinary clinic knew from its research that within three to eight months of moving into a new area, pet owners will look for a clinic to care for or board their pet. Because the clinic wanted to be viewed as a neighborhood vet, it determined that creating top-of-mind awareness with new homeowners and renters within a 20-mile radius was vital to its growth. The first step in narrowing down the list was to identify people living in apartment complexes where pets were allowed. Then, based on demographic information of the typical pet owner, the list was further narrowed by a mailing list company to also include homeowners. The initial list was made up of those who had moved into the area within the last three months. It was then updated monthly only with those renters or homeowners who were new to their residences. The clinic sent a few hundred cards a month. The campaign featured a series of eight monthly post cards mailed in a predetermined sequence.

> **Direct mail has gotten a bad rap because too many businesses do it so poorly. When done right, it can be a powerful component of a marketing program that helps your business stand out among competitors, while serving as a steady reminder to your ideal market that you exist.**

The mailer side of the oversized post cards posed questions to pique the interest of the recipient. They included: "Pets are people too, right?" "Is your dog your family's best friend?" "Is your cat your purrrfect companion?" "Is your pet on the go wherever you go?" The promotional side included two special offers. This manageable and targeted campaign fostered growth adding new families who choose this clinic as their neighborhood vet.

Personal vs. Postmarked: Address the card with the recipient's name and be sure the name is spelled correctly. Addressing a piece to "current resident" is impersonal and screams that it has been mailed to a massive list. Place an actual stamp on the piece instead of running it through a meter. You can now create custom stamps with the post office, and some businesses have done this effectively to reinforce their brand image. Another nice touch is to use a wax seal on the envelope. Businesses are also having a great deal of success using resources such as Send Out Cards for one-to-one mailings. It allows personal touches to be incorporated into the preparation of the message and its imagery.

Variable Data vs. Mailing Labels: Technology has enabled direct mail to be truly directed to its recipient with personalized precision for a powerful impact. Printing companies can now digitally generate personalized text within the graphics so the direct mail piece appears to have been written specifically for the recipient. This is known as variable data generation. By using a person's name in the text and emphasizing their personal preferences, recipients are often blown away by how well the business appears to understand who they are and what is important to them. The quality of personal computer laser printers has also enabled businesses to produce highly effective and targeted mailing pieces in-house a few hundred at a time. This cuts down on the cost and also allows customization of the message to each recipient. Technology is also being used in conjunction with direct mail to entice a person to visit a personalized website with the person's name in the URL. Always be sure to include your website on your direct mail piece with a special incentive for going online.

Ongoing vs. Hit or Miss: A direct mail campaign should be a series to be effective. Instead of trying to put everything in one post card and mailing it to a massive list, do a series of post cards to smaller, more-targeted lists. Introduce your offerings in a more focused manner, presenting one key advantage of value in each card, the campaign should be no less than three post cards and can be up to 12. The frequency depends on your overall strategy. A monthly mailing complemented by other marketing initiatives can garner great returns. Or you may prefer a more intense series of back-to-back mailings over a few weeks. It always goes back to the buying patterns of your target market in conjunction with what you are offering. Another thing to consider is doing two types of mailings. For instance, there can be a promotional post card series that introduces specific offerings. Then a newsletter or bulletin can be mailed that offers more content and information of value.

Getting Creative: If you decide to send a sealed mailing of some kind, getting creative can result in a higher impact. But it can be costly on a per-piece basis. When determining to make this level of investment, be clear what you hope to gain and achieve with the mailing. Is it to create awareness? Is it to showcase your creativity and innovative ability? Also, what action do you want the recipient to take?

Top Secret

A nonwoven materials manufacturing company wanted to gain attention and attendance at the official opening of its new research and development facility, which included a ribbon cutting, tour and reception. To create excitement, a package was sent featuring a black miniature briefcase stamped "TOP SECRET." Inside was a pair of binoculars, an invitation and a tape recorder. The invitation invited the recipient to play the recorder. The theme from 'Mission Impossible' began to play, and the recording proceeded to state the individual person's name and their mission, "should they choose to accept." The packages were sent overnight. With customers, prospects, and key trade media contacts located all over the country, the cost of attendance for a majority of the individuals being invited included travel and lodging. Spending nearly $100 per piece seemed inconsequential compared to the investment required of attendees. The memorable and personalized mailing was a home run that garnered lots of media coverage and strong attendance by key customers and prospects.

•   •   •

Direct mail done right can truly bring impressive returns on your investment. Before you dismiss it, get strategic about it. It can be the perfect supplement to your core marketing initiatives to bring in sales.

46
Income Streams

The agility of a small business is never more tested than in challenging times. It's what has made entrepreneurship a driving force behind any economic recovery. Many entrepreneurs say – in hindsight – that a challenge or downturn was the best thing that ever happened to their business. It made them get more resourceful and creative. As the saying goes, "What doesn't kill you will make you stronger."

From Services to Products: As we discussed in Secret #11, many service businesses add products to their mix of offerings as a means of diversifying their income streams while better serving their customers. But adding products does not necessarily mean you make them. For example, an acupuncturist or massage therapist might add herbal treatment products and nutritional supplements to their offerings. A spa that adds pampering products for use at home gives clients the opportunity to browse and buy while waiting for services.

From Products to Consulting: If you have acquired a specialized expertise around the products you provide, add consulting to your offerings. A supplier and installer of a market-exclusive energy-efficient insulation product made it his business to know the entire realm of energy-efficient options available. He was so respected that industry peers often sought him out for his knowledge and guidance. Seeing a void in the market, he added consulting to his business offerings for other professionals as well as for consumers.

Multiple Momentum

Since its founding in 2004, a marketing services consultant enjoyed a steadily growing business and a solid reputation. But the reality was she was the company. She realized that for her to grow her sales beyond current capacity and to be able to eventually retire, she had to build her business in a different way. She also knew she had to develop several income streams to provide residual income without her needing to be physically present. For many years, she dreamed of writing fiction. She had started on a manuscript in the late 1990s, but considered it a hobby. But in 2006, she determined the time had come to set her multiple income plan in motion, and her first novel was published in 2007. Because of her marketing prowess, her first book was a success. This resulted in a multi-book contract and inquiries from other authors wanting to know her secrets to successful promotion. So she entered the nonfiction arena with books that showed others how to market theirs. In the meantime, she increased the offerings of her marketing business beyond consulting services to include teleseminars, webinars, professional speaking, and packaged programs and products targeted to solo entrepreneurs. By building a solid base of five income streams, this savvy marketer saw 40 percent growth in 2009 and is seeing the same level of growth in 2010. The consulting portion of her business has gone from representing 100 percent of her revenues to 25 percent, with the rest coming from her other four income streams.

> *The best way to recession-proof your business is to develop at least five income streams that are not reliant on one another to be sustained. If you can accomplish this type of cash flow, then you won't know that a downturn has occurred except through hearing others' woes.*

From Cost Plus to Consulting Plus: In certain pricing models, service and expertise are built into the mark-up of the products sold. When times are good, and people are spending, there is no concern as sales flow in. But when economic times get lean, you may find yourself investing a great deal of upfront time into products only to see the project put on indefinite hold. In working with clients, interior designers traditionally invested a great deal of time and energy in selecting fabrics, furniture and other accessories, expecting to make their profit when clients approved the design and placed an order. But savvy design professionals now charge an upfront design fee for the creative portion of their work, with it being applied against purchases. This works well in creating cash flow for time spent while reinforcing the value of the creative aspect of their services. Some perceptive designers are also finding opportunities in advising homeowners on how to rearrange their existing furnishings. With a few new accessories and accents, they can totally refresh a room without spending thousands of dollars.

From Promotional to Professional Speaking: Business owners and their top managers who have effectively established an area of specialized expertise can leverage their stature as authorities to become paid speakers. What you used to do for free as a way to promote your company can become a new source of income. Because these speaking fees are paid directly to you, you can draw less salary from your company (with no decrease in personal income) and reinvest it in the business.

From Associate to Affiliate Programs: To increase the power of your referral network, consider establishing an affiliate program where you pay a commission for any referral that converts to a sale. In doing so, you have created an additional income stream for companies who already consider your business worth promoting to others.

From Creative Services to Support Services: When money gets tight, the creative services industry particularly feels the pinch. This is when being resourceful can prove its weight in gold. Take a step back to see how your ideal market is still spending money. Then figure out ways how you can meet those needs with additional specialized or support services. Spending never stops entirely – it just shifts or gets re-prioritized. Understand the priorities, and sales can be yours.

Panoramic View

An outdoor living design-and-build firm anticipated the slowdown in the high-end home market because fewer new construction and renovation permits were being issued. Specializing in nature-inspired outdoor living spaces beyond just basic landscaping, the company had built a solid reputation and was considered the premier choice in the marketplace. The owners knew they could secure a meaningful share of the work still available. However, the decline in permits meant a decline in opportunities for these elaborate projects. Sales would inevitably decline if the firm only relied on the design and build aspect of the business. The owners knew they had a limited timeframe to assess opportunities and proactively shift so sales could be generated from other

*sources. While homeowners of high-end homes were not
investing in new designs and plantings, they still took
great pride in their properties and wanted them cared for
and maintained. Therefore, the firm's landscape
maintenance services began to pick up momentum. In
addition, with so many homes for sale, ones with curb
appeal had a greater likelihood of selling. The firm
began offering outdoor staging with simple, yet appealing
low-cost improvements to exterior landscaping to increase
a property's appeal to a prospective buyer. While other
landscape design firms struggled to survive, this firm
kept 20 crews busy and saw 15 percent growth during one
of the most challenging years in the residential
landscaping industry.*

From List to Subscribers: After your business gains a large following because of its expertise and resources, consider charging customers a subscription fee for regularly receiving specialized information or insights. The fee can be assessed monthly, quarterly, or annually and gives subscribers access to proprietary information and exclusive reports.

From Physical Training to Virtual Training: With webinars and virtual meetings occurring daily over the Internet, companies that once offered training at physical locations now offer Web-based training at a fraction of the cost. In some cases, the training can be provided as a pre-paid download and attendees can takes the course or workshop at their convenience.

From Trainer to Training Systems: Although not a good investment decision as stated in Secret #9, many companies cut training budgets during economic downturns. Smart training companies are responding to this challenge by providing train-the-trainer programs and systems that let clients conduct these programs in-house by themselves. These companies continue to offer options while their competitors wait things out.

•   •   •

Ingenuity is what makes entrepreneurship such a powerful influence on every aspect of the economy. If your current business model has reached a plateau or if sales are declining, take a step back. Determine where you can create other income streams to fulfill your mission and give customers more reasons to do business with you in new and innovative ways

CRISP PRINCIPLE: FORMULAS FOR SUCCESS

47
C+R+I+S+P = $ales

As mentioned in Secret #44, advertising is not a core marketing initiative for growth companies, but rather a strategic supplemental initiative. Before you consider any form of advertising, be sure you have the five core marketing initiatives in place on an ongoing basis. The five initiatives, which I call the CRISP Principle Power of Five, are: Customer Relations, Referral Relations, Internet Presence, Strategic Involvements and Public Relations.

In the book's preface, "CRISP Principle: The Study," you learned that these five initiatives are the key components to business marketing success. They must be at the core of any marketing plan. I conducted the study to gain further insight and documentation of what works and what doesn't. I wasn't just proving a theory, I was attempting to validate a way to take a small business to market. In Secrets #13-43, I gave you specific ideas, concepts and guidance within each of these five core initiatives that growth businesses successfully implement. You may have already begun putting some of these concepts and ideas into action. Fabulous! But are you feeling overwhelmed by all the options and how to decide which ones to implement first?

Read on! In this section, I will share the real power of these five initiatives when used together in various combinations. Whatever the current state of your business, this section will help you prioritize which tactical areas to focus on first, based on your available resources of money, time, people and technology. You will have a clearer idea of which of these "formulas" for success is right for your business. First, let's recap what each of these initiatives entails.

C = Power of Customer Relations: In the Customer Relations section, you learned about mastering mindshare, relationships versus transactions, as well as every aspect of serving your customers: connecting with them, rewarding and informing them, personally communicating with them, segmenting and targeting them, celebrating and recognizing them, and finally, wowing them. Will doing all these things keep you busy with customer referrals alone? Yes and no. Many businesses grow by having highly satisfied customers who provide them with regular referrals and repeat business. This can last for years. However, the problem occurs when the business owner decides it's time for the business to expand beyond its current geographic market or market segment. If there's a market shift, like an economic downturn, it may be necessary to go after an entirely different market for survival. Before the current recession, many businesses were profitable with customer referrals alone bringing in new sales. Then the bottom fell out. With no other marketing initiatives – or even a strategy – to anticipate this possibility, these businesses struggled. Many are no longer in business. Relying solely on your customers to generate sales is no different than relying on advertising as your only marketing tactic. You must create a multi-faceted marketing engine where your customers are just one of five pistons firing up the opportunities.

R = Power of Referral Relations: In the Referral Relations section you learned about gaining referrals beyond customers to include your competition, cross promotions and circles of influence. You don't need a referral relations program with your customers. Because of your customer relationship initiatives, they should already be willingly and enthusiastically sharing their experiences doing business with you with others. We found in our study that most stagnant or no-growth businesses don't utilize referral relations at all. One reason is that they only look to customers for referrals. They also don't understand the powerful ripple effect a strong referral relations program can have on their business. When a company adds a referral relations program to its mix, it creates the potential for an independent sales force promoting the business without the overhead.

> *In the CRISP Principle study, companies with more than 50 percent growth over a three to five year period used multiple levels of all five of the CRISP Principles in their marketing strategy. This is significant since this growth occurred in the aftermath of 9-11 and the economic downturn in 2002-2003.*

I = Power of the Internet: High-growth companies use the Internet daily for communications and operations and to obtain resources and information. And so do almost every consumer in the marketplace. In the Internet Presence section, you learned the power of using your company's Internet presence as a virtual receptionist and business tool. You also learned the importance of having a dynamic website and of developing an Internet presence beyond it. You gained insight about the power of optimization and why you need to stop relying on phone books. You have also probably noticed how the Internet is interwoven into the other four initiatives. For instance, I recommended you use e-mail and social media to communicate with your customers and referral network. As you become involved in activities outside your business, these involvements will often be recognized on another entity's web site, which may also provide links to your site. The media has been forced onto the Internet in a big way so successful exposure through public relations will inevitably end up being viewed by qualified prospects online. Now you can see why the Internet truly is at the center of your marketing as well as at the center of the CRISP Principle.

S = Power of Strategic Involvements: In the Strategic Involvements section, you learned about purposeful affiliations, trade collaborations, charitable giving, charitable causes, strategic relationships, sponsorships and the importance of fostering a sense of community. You should select an involvement based on its ability to put you in direct contact with your ideal target markets or those who can refer you to them, as well as to gain resources and support for your business. You now understand the differences between being a member, participant, involved, and being strategically involved. Chances are, you have changed some of your involvements as a result. Or, if you haven't been involved in any group or activity outside your business, you are now determined to get involved in the right organizations in the right way for the right reasons.

P = Power of Public Relations: You learned that growth-oriented companies use public relations to proactively seek opportunities, position themselves as expert resources, host events with a cause, take leadership roles in their community or marketplace, and pursue awards and recognition. You read examples of how the power of the press can create even more opportunities for your business to gain exposure and credibility. You now know how to begin a media relations program including how to prepare news releases, target and send them for maximum impact.

•   •   •

After you finish the book, I urge you to go back and re-read all the success stories highlighted in each of the chapters. You will realize that although just one type of CRISP initiative or strategy is highlighted, the featured company concurrently implemented several others. Once you have developed a strategy, the secret to success lies in learning how to make these five initiatives powerfully work together and build off each other. CRISP Principle: Power of Five is your strategy put into action. Working together, these initiatives bring synergy to your marketing and operational efforts. They create a momentum that enables your business to not only ride out the storms, but to rise to the top.

Because the CRISP Principle: Power of Five works so well, it might work too well. You could run into problems if you implement it without any operational infrastructure in place to serve the additional business. If you are unable to deliver on your promises, problems with customer relations and satisfaction could occur. Therefore, it is best for existing businesses to incorporate the initiatives in phases to manage growth in balance with the capacity of the business.

48

$(R + S) + (I + P) = GO$

If you are preparing to launch your business and are already developing a marketing strategy, congratulations! Most start-up businesses don't even think about marketing until after they have opened. But they need to be thinking about it long before so eager customers walk in the door the first day of business. This is what makes the CRISP Principle so powerful for a start-up business. Certain aspects of the CRISP Principle can be put into action well ahead of an official opening.

R+S = Pre-Launch Strategy: Before launching your business, you can implement the referral relations and strategic involvements components of the CRISP Principle. As described in Secret #22, you and your key team members should identify key influencers or providers to your target market and introduce your business to them well before it opens. Share ideas on how you can work together, as well as your plans to send opportunities their way. By identifying both direct and indirect competitors, you can connect with the indirect ones and emphasize how you are different and how you can cross refer or join together to serve your customers. When I decided to relocate my business to the Southeast, I identified mid-sized advertising and marketing agencies serving larger companies. I introduced my company's full-service capabilities as a resource to refer small businesses. These indirect competitors were an immediate source of referrals as they realized their services were too expensive for small businesses. They appreciated being able to refer them to another full-service source. As you manage these one-on-one relationships, identify strategic groups to join. Participate in their events and activities and share the anticipation of your opening. This can give you an opportunity to identify a worthwhile cause or community involvement to support as a component of your opening. If you are a retail location, surrounding merchants can be a part of a countdown to your opening as a promotion to create excitement.

Inspired by the Best

A bridal and formalwear boutique was planning to open in a posh part of town and wanted to make their store the destination of choice within a 100-mile radius. They secured some exclusive designer labels and had no real competitors within 30 miles. The owners knew they needed a strong referral network to accomplish their goal. Before opening, they hosted a private soiree inviting everyone who served the bridal industry within their geographic market. The formal invitation was a thank you to the Best of the Best for inspiring the business owners to open the store. They said they were honored to become a part of an industry all about new beginnings, celebrations and relationships. The reception was a huge success, and the boutique captured the respect and loyalty of an impressed group of vendors who had never been shown appreciation this way before. Those attending were included in the boutique's bridal resource book that customers referenced in the downtime during fittings. These colleagues, in turn, became an ever-flowing source of referrals. Just 12 months after opening, the boutique was named Best of the Best by a local magazine over other bridal shops that had been in the region for decades.

> *Referral relations are critical to a start-up business because you don't have any customers yet to generate referrals. Building a referral network to encourage prospects to check out your business should begin months before your doors open.*

(R+S)+(I+P) = Initial Launch: Once your referral relationships and strategic involvements are in full swing, add an Internet presence and public relations activity to the mix. Creating a viral buzz a couple of weeks before you open through social media sites can build excitement. Sending a news release prior to the opening also builds a buzz. Offering an exclusive story to a key publication could garner a feature story rather than an announcement. If there is a unique news or trend tie-in, all the better. When announcing your business opening, it is smart not to announce everything about the business in the first release. Hold back some information for follow-up releases so the media gets a sense your newly opened business is making things happen. With business already flowing in because of your pre-launch activities, you can hold an official grand opening or appreciation event a few months later. Leverage it by tying it to a charitable cause. The key is to build momentum well before you open and then keep the momentum going.

Seeing is Believing

A husband and wife optometry team identified where they wanted to live and build a practice. Their chosen community had immense growth opportunity and would be a great place to raise a family. However, the couple was starting a practice in a community with optometrists who had been in business for 20 and 30 years. They began to strategically plan their practice opening more than a year in advance. They hired a marketing consultant who helped them effectively introduce their practice to the community. Part of the strategy was identifying opportunities to be involved in the community in a variety of ways prior to opening. The doctors also focused on building a strong referral network among those who served the families they hoped would be their patients. Several months before opening their practice, the doctors embraced this strategy by participating in free vision screenings with the school, business groups, the Rotary and community events. This was easy for them because they both had a strong belief in community service. They made time to introduce themselves to merchants, healthcare providers and business people in the community. They shared what they planned to do and asked how they could help other businesses in the area. As the official opening drew near, they prepared their website to go live and sent timely news releases about their planned events and charitable involvements. Their initial goals for their practice were very conservative, and they hoped for a few patients to launch their practice. But thanks to their efforts before opening, they had appointments booked on their first day. Since opening in 2004, they have continued their community involvement and are now considered the premier family eye care practice in the area. They are often the first optometrists recommended when people seek referrals from residents. The practice has grown from 825 patients in its impressive first year to 3,668 patients in 2009. Their current tagline proclaims "You'll see, we care." An entire marketplace not only sees it, but experiences how much they care.

•   •   •

With referral relations, Internet marketing, strategic involvements and public relations working in unison, you can quickly implement the full CRISP Principle as customers come into your business eager to check it out because of all the build-up. If you start your business with the CRISP Principle as your marketing model, you will be assured that your money and time are spent in the most valuable and beneficial ways possible.

49

C + R + I + S = VSF

Every business owner wishes for sales to just walk through the door without any effort on their part. If customer referrals are the only way you get new business other than your own direct efforts, the pressure on you is immense. Add the fact that you also have to fulfill the service or move the product, and it can be downright overwhelming. So what happens? You service for a while and sell for a while, then service for a while and then sell for a while.

When you are on that rollercoaster, chances are you don't do either activity well. Sales that just happen would indeed be a dream come true. Well, that can happen if you put a virtual sales force behind your business. By adding the CRISP initiatives one by one, you will soon see sales rolling in, and you can focus more on ensuring that services and products get out the door.

C+ R = Beyond Customer: You now understand the power of building a referral network, so it should be your first area of focus. With a referral network touting your business along with customers, you are increasing the likelihood that someone inquiring will be receiving multiple recommendations of your company. Once a solid referral network becomes a standard part of your business, you will wonder why you ever totally relied on customer referrals alone.

C+R+I = Beyond Walls: Often when businesses rely solely on customer referrals, they either don't have a website, or it's a marginal one. It is time to move beyond the walls of your business and enter the world of the Internet to unleash its business-generating power. Combine a service and information-oriented website with social media and optimization enhancements. When someone searches for your product or service, let the Internet work its magic in pointing qualified buyers your way.

Car Chicks

An automotive consulting company decided to take on the entire automotive sales industry when it determined to specifically focus on and serve the female car buyer. The female ownership wanted to create a more positive

buying experience for women, helping them avoid the
hassles, time and frustrations with the negotiating
process. It would be a company of women helping women
in a man's world. From the onset, a strong brand image
was developed and positioning that got attention due to
the niche focus. From the website to its branded vehicles,
it was clear there was a new car buying resource in
town. Integral to the company's success in gaining
clients was in aligning with women's groups on the
target market side and trade groups on the service
industry side to gain referrals and interested prospects.
Once clients were secured, the ownership knew their
solutions-based and consulting
approach would realize more
client referrals, while industry
referrals continued to stream
in. Determined not to be
viewed as brokers, they worked
cooperatively with car dealers
and gained respect throughout
the industry as a team of
consultants that create a win-
win for clients and suppliers
alike. Their web presence
continued to grow and evolve
with the business from being a
promotional site to offering
resources, business
opportunities and then social
media links, a blog, and more
to continue to stay in step with
how the market was resourcing information. To add
further credibility and to continue to expand the
company's circle of influence, one owner became involved
in racing and the high performance arena. Throughout
the company's growth, the owners meticulously
documented and put procedures around their processes
and approach so it could be replicable as a licensed
distributor offering. In 2006, they offered their first
distributorship. Their reputation as "Car Chicks" who
know their stuff has not only caught the respect of

> **In the CRISP Principle
> study, growth companies
> received referrals from
> mere acquaintances or
> people they had never
> met. This is when you
> know you have a virtual
> sales engine behind your
> business when referrals
> happen any time, any
> where and even when you
> are not there.**

women, but also the industry and busy executive men. Their business client base is now a mix of men and women. By 2009, distributors were operational in five states from the west coast to the southeast. The company's virtual sales force continues to build its base of satisfied clients as new distributorships are being identified.

C+R+I+S = Beyond Owner: With your customers being wowed, a referral network touting your business and an Internet presence providing online exposure, you can then select some strategic involvements to elevate your company image and present your leadership skills to the marketplace. Once you have strategically integrated customer relations, referral relations, the Internet and strategic involvements into your business, the flood gates will open with qualified prospects wanting to do business with you.

• • •

You'll know your business has reached its stride when you no longer feel stressed about building your business, but instead are enjoying it. You are no longer one of several companies potential customers consider. Instead, you are recommended as the only place to go by an entire network of individuals. Business owners who "get" the power of building a virtual sales force for their business know the powerful connections you make everyday, virtually and in person, mean big business to the small business.

50

$$C + I^3 + P = NL$$

As business owners grow their businesses, there is often a period when they feel stuck. Everything is going well, and business is steady, but getting to that next level is elusive. When taking your business to a new level, it typically means re-evaluating where it is currently and building a strategy to get you to where you want to be. Chances are you are stuck because you are still using your old strategy. You need insight. You need to assess your image. You need to take a look at your business with a different set of eyes.

C+ I = Customer Driven Insight: Start by talking to your existing customer base for insight and perspective. The value they bring to your decision-making is priceless. Many businesses think that asking customers questions may be intrusive. But I know from direct experience they are delighted to be respected and valued for what they can contribute. You should also seek insights about any new markets you are considering adding. It can also be very useful to leverage any referral relationships you have to seek interviews with their customers who reflect your new market focus.

Some things you will want to know are:

- Perceptions of your business in the marketplace and industry
- Perceptions of your company name, logo brand and image
- Who they perceive to be your competitors and how you compare
- Most valued capabilities and products
- Greatest opportunities for growth in their opinion
- Awareness of your services and products
- Preferences and insight to products or services under consideration
- Most and least impressive aspect of people
- Most and least impressive aspect of service and support
- Most and least impressive aspect of way of doing business
- Most and least impressive aspect of knowledge and experience
- Ways to better serve them and grow with them
- Concerns and possible challenges to consider
- Areas to improve

The best and most convenient way to accomplish this phase is with scheduled telephone interviews. Conduct them at times convenient for the customers so they will be fully engaged in answering the questions and offering feedback. It is important that whoever does the interviews does not interact with the customer on a regular basis. It should not be you. Hire a firm or an individual to do it for you. Have the results compiled so you won't be tempted to single out feedback or dismiss it because it comes from a particular customer. All feedback is relevant and must be considered.

1 + 1 = Branding & the Internet: After you've gained these new insights, you must look at your company's brand image and revisit your website. Adjust the content with the new or expanded focus area. In some cases, a new company name may be warranted. Or you may need an updated logo or a more defined overall branding strategy. Once you have defined your brand, immediately integrate it into your Internet presence. This is critical to reintroducing your company to existing markets and introducing it to new ones.

Generations & Growing

A certified financial planner practicing since 1979 had built a solid reputation with her clientele. Yet a marketplace with immense opportunity was not aware she was an option. While proud to claim steady growth from client referrals alone since establishing heu own firm in 1990, she was ready to take her practice to a higher level. It was important to her to control the firm's growth so it would not impede on her or her associates' ability to serve current clients at the level to which they had grown accustomed. She hired a branding development firm to help her with this strategic initiative and gained insight from her clients to confirm the direction she was heading. As a result, she learned through her clients' eyes what they considered most distinctive about her firm. A branding and marketing strategy was developed that reflected her unique approach

> *Growth-oriented business owners are continuously revisiting their strategies to confirm they are in alignment with the changing times and their target market needs. They seek insight on a regular basis so when an opportunity is identified, they can quickly shift and pursue its full potential.*

*and process in working with clients. In addition, a
tagline and domain address was inspired by the fact
many of her clients represented several generations
within a family because of their long-time trust and
confidence in her. Client feedback had also affirmed that
a website was a much-needed addition. The website
included the story behind the firm's brand, philosophy,
experience and capabilities. Her Internet presence
quickly became a valued tool for clients to use in their
referrals and was a resource in accessing and reviewing
their accounts in real time. A review of competitors
uncovered that most did not conduct public relations
programs. This inspired the savvy financial planner to
learn how to execute an ongoing public relations effort.
After attending a workshop, she and an associate put the
plan into action with consistent and ongoing results. Her
firm realized double-digit growth that continued during
the economic debacle of 2008 and 2009 when many of her
competitors faltered. Her astute attentiveness to clients'
risk tolerances and her focus on trending and financial
analysis resulted in protecting her clients from the
disappointing losses many others experienced. She was
recognized as one of the Top 25 Women in Achievement
for company growth in 2009 and as a Five Star Wealth
Manager for Client Satisfaction in her market area.
Deeply satisfied as her firm continues to flourish, she
proves the value of a solid marketing approach while
helping clients meet their needs by creating financial
strategies for life.*

C + I³ + P = Public Awareness: Once your branding strategy is in place and your revamped website has gone live, launch an awareness campaign through media relations and other public relations tactics. Announcing your expanded market focus or company name change in an initial news release can be followed by opportunities to speak or be a resource on trends you discovered in your customer research. Strategically releasing news about products or capabilities in phases to the media will create an interest in your company and its progress.

•   •   •

With realigned customers, strategic insights, a solid image, a strong Internet presence and a PR effort that reintroduces you to the marketplace, you can then concentrate on building referral and strategic relationships to send you further along to the next level. This formula guarantees a well orchestrated re-entry into the marketplace meticulously designed to bring growth to your business.

About the Author

Sherré DeMao is passionate about helping entrepreneurs prosper in life and in business and has dedicated her 25-year career to this purpose. She is founder and Chief Marketeer of SLD Unlimited Marketing/PR, Inc., a full-service branding, marketing, consulting and strategy firm she established in 1984. Sherré helps owners of start-up and small-to-medium-sized companies become savvier managers and marketers by providing innovative operational and marketing guidance, solutions and services.

Her firm's creative solutions have won numerous awards including Telly, ProAd, PICA, Addy and IABC Crown awards. Her dedication to small business and her entrepreneurial know-how has earned her local, regional and national recognition. In 2004, the National Republican Congressional Committee honored her with a National Leadership Award for her small business advocacy. As chair of a national procurement task force formed by the National Association of Women Business Owners (NAWBO), Sherré co-authored a white paper on federal government contracting practices with small, women-owned and minority-owned business. Published by NAWBO in February 2006, the paper included 34 recommendations to federal agencies, which were presented on Capitol Hill to legislative subcommittees relevant to the procurement agenda. The paper is still used as a resource today. These efforts were among the reasons Sherré was recognized in 2006 as a Small Business Woman Champion by the U.S. Small Business Administration. In 2007, she was named among the 50 Most Enterprising Women in North America by *Enterprising Women Magazine*.

As an entrepreneurial business expert, Sherré frequently provides commentary and perspective to local, regional and national media. She writes a monthly "Savvy Business Owner" column in *Business Today* and is a contributing writer with articles appearing in *Enterprising Women Magazine*, *Women Entrepreneur*, Entrepreneur.com, Business Insider, FoxBusiness.com, and Yahoo Small Business. Her first book, *Me, Myself & Inc. – A Synergized World, An Energized Business, Living Your Ultimate Life*, was named a Top Business Shelf pick by Midwest Book Review in 2009.

Acknowledgements

The following companies are cited as examples and success stories throughout this book. Many of these companies I worked with personally, while others I had the pleasure of interviewing as a result of being impressed in my research by their ability to put a multitude of the 50 secrets into practice.

AcuCare Clinic
Abe Rummage, L.Ac, LMBT
www.acucareclinic.com

Advanced Family Eye Care
Dr. Amanda Barker-Assell
Dr. Micheal Assell
www.seeadvanced.com

AdzZoo
Pat Volgerson
www.adzzoo.com

Altman Initiative Group, Inc
Business Success Institute
Denise Altman, President
www.altmaninitiative.com
www.business-successinstitute.com

Anatech LTD
George Barr, Founder/President
BioMedFlex, LLC
BioMedFlex-Spine, LLC
OrthoMedFlex, LLC
BioMedInnovations, LLC
Smart Profusion, LLC
VasoConnect, LLC
www.anatechltdusa.com

Avantgarde Translations, Inc.
Memuna Williams, President, United States
Isata Jones-Stanley, President, Canada
www.avantgardetranslations.com

Ballantine Insurance & Financial Services Inc.
Mary Beth Ballantine, ChFC
www.marybeth.cc

Banco de la Gente
Manuel Rey, President
www.bancodelagente.com

Ben & Jerry's Homemade, Inc
Jostein Solheim, CEO
Ben Cohen, Co-Founder, Chair of the Board
Jerry Greenfield, Co-Founder, Vice-Chair of the Board
www.benandjerrys.com

Boyle Consulting Engineers, PLLC
Chuck Boyle, PE, Managing Principal
www.boyleconsulting.com

Car Chick, Inc.
dba Women's Automotive Solutions, Inc.
Michelle Lundy, Founder/CEO
LeeAnn Shuttuck, Chief Car Chick
www.womensautomotivesolutions.com

C Design Inc
Robert C. Crane Jr., AIA, Founder/Managing Principal
www.cdesigninc.com

CCS Cartridge & Document Innovations
Formerly Carolina Cartridge Systems, Inc.
Sharon Summers, President/CEO
www.ccsinside.com

Carolina Foam Solutions, Inc.
Todd Nichols, President
Scott Nichols, Vice President
www.carolinafoamsolutions.com

Chien Associates, LLC
Chia-Li Chien, Founder/Chief Strategist
www.chialichien.com

Clear Align
Angelique X. Irvin, President/CEO
www.clearalign.com

Clickcom, Inc.
John DiCristo, CEO
Nick DiCristo, Vice President
Jon Szymanski, President
www.clickcom.com

College Hunks Hauling Junk
Steve Nickels, Director of Franchise
Support
www.1800junkusa.com

Comprehensive Benefits Solutions
Ron Stromple, President
www.cbsse.com

Coogan's Landscape, Inc
Tom Coogan
www.cooganslandscape.com

Cox Schepp Construction, Inc.
Robert Andrew Cox, Chairman/CEO
Jim Schepp, Vice Chairman/Chief
Administrative Officer
www.coxschepp.com

Dolf Dunn Wealth Management
Adolphus W. Dunn III, CFP, CPA, CPWA,
AEP
Managing Principal, Private Wealth Manager,
LPL Financial
www.dolfdunn.com

Dreamspinner Communications, Inc.
Gail Z. Martin, President
www.dreamspinnercommunications.com

DS Audio Video, Inc.
Scott Campbell, Owner
www.ds-audiovideo.com

Duncan Williams, Inc, - Charlotte
Barry Ezarsky, Manager
www.duncanw.com

Fishing with Gus
Captain Gus Gustafson
www.lakenormanstriperfishing.com

Freedom Animal Hospital
Margurette Staley, Owner
www.freedomanimalhospital.com

**Goodwill Industries of the Southern
Piedmont**
Bo Hussey, VP of Marketing and
Communications
www.goodwillsp.org

Google, Inc.
Eric Schmidt, CEO
Larry Page, Co-Founder, President,
Products
Sergey Brin, Co-Founder, President,
Technology
www.google.com

Grey & Company, Inc.
Mitzi T. Grey, RNC, MEd, President
www.greyandco.com

**HAMCO Manufacturing &
Distributing, LLC**
George Hare, General Manager
Gene Brittain, Senior Cost Accountant
Gary Isom, Plant Manager
Elaina Phillips, Customer Service Manager
www.hamco-products.com

HomeInstead Charlotte
Les Farnum, Co-Owner
Roberta Borsella Farnum, Co-Owner
www.homeinsteadcharlotte.com

iCore Networks, Inc.
Steve Canton, Chairman/CEO
Shayda Sadeghian, Executive Assistant to
CEO
www.icore.com

Integra Staffing & Search, Inc.
Michelle Fish, CEO
Robert Fish, CFO
Izzy Justice, President/CEO
Bankston Partners, Founder
Diversity Forum
www.integrastaffing.com
www.bankstoneq.com
www.thediversityforum.org

Joyce Foods, Inc.
Ron Joyce, President/CEO
www.joycefoods.com

Just For You Salon & Spa
Vi Phantirath, Owner/Manager

Kaleidoscope Business Options, Inc.
Mary Bruce, President
www.kboptions.com

Keller Williams Realty International
Gary Keller, Co-Founder/Chairman of the
Board
Jay Papasan, VP of Publishing/Executive
Editor
Dave Jenks, VP of Research and
Development
www.kw.com

Shift, By Gary Keller with Dave Jenks and
Jay Papasan
McGraw Hill, Inc.
MH Professional
www.mhprofessional.com

The Lily Rose
Karis Kremers, Co-founder
Denise Lyerly, Co-founder
Susan Sabatini, Co-founder
www.lilyrosebridal.com

Metro GreenScape
Darin Brockelbank, Outdoor Living
Specialist
Heather Brockelbank, Chief Designer
www.metrogreenscape.com

Michael Port & Associates, LLC
Michael Port, President
Booked Solid University
www.bookyourselfsolid.com

Mission Essential Personnel, Inc.
Chris Taylor, CEO
Marc Peltier, COO
Sunil Ramchand, Chief of Staff
www.missionep.com

Nannies4hire.com
Candi Wingate, President
Care4hire.com
Babysitters4hire.com
www.nannies4hire.com

Oompa Toys, Inc.
Jason Oliver, COO
Milanie Cleere, CEO
www.oompa.com

Peoples Bank, North Carolina
Tony Wolfe, President/CEO
www.peoplesbanknc.com

Pilates Studio at the Lake
Carrie Jacobs, Owner/Founder
www.pilatesstudioatthelake.com

Polymer Group, Inc.
www.polymergroupinc.com

Preferred Financial Strategies, Inc.
Sara I. Seasholtz, CFP®, President
www.financialstrategiesforlife.com

Quality Propane, Inc.
Terry Rudisill, President
Vickie Rudisill, Vice President
www.qualitypropaneinc.com

Rahe Lynne Clothier
Lynne Byrd, Owner/President
www.rahelynne.com

Saebo, Inc.
Henry Hoffman, Co-founder/President
www.saebo.com

Salvin Dental Specialties, Inc
Bob Salvin, Founder/CEO
William Simmons, President
Greg Slayton, Vice President
www.salvin.com

Sensibly Chic Interior Design
Barbara Green, The Design Diva
www.sensiblychic.biz

Signature Healthcare, PLLC
Dr. Jordan Lipton
Dr. Elizabeth Perry
Dr. Bryan Woodward
www.signaturehealthcarellc.com

SLD Unlimited Marketing/PR, Inc.
Sherré DeMao, President/Chief Marketeer
www.sldunlimited.com

Snug Seat, Inc.
Kirk MacKenzie, President
Steve Scribner, Vice President, Sales
www.snugseat.com

Sodoma Law
Nicole Sodoma, Attorney
sodomalaw.com

SPARK Publications, Inc.
Fabi Preslar, President
www.sparkpublications.com

Spivey Construction Company, Inc.
Willis Spivey, President
www.spiveyinc.com

Talbot Corporate Services, Inc.
Paul Talbot, Owner

Terri Bennett Enterprises, Inc.
Terri Bennett, Vice President of Production and Content
www.terribennett.com
www.doyourpart.com

Tribble Creative Group, Inc.
Mary Tribble, President
Cassie Brown, Director of Events
www.tribblecreativegroup.com

Universal Rubber Products, Inc.
Robert Cotton Davis, President
Bob Davis, Vice President
Emily Davis, Operations Manager
www.universalrubber.com

Village Pet Animal Hospital
Venus Painter, Office Manager
Dr. Warren Moretz, Founder
www.villagepetvet.com

VisionCor, Inc.
Sherry Barretta, CEO
www.visioncor.com

Xtreme Consulting Group, Inc.
Greg Rankich, CEO/President/Co-Founder
Tony Richardson, Chief Technology Officer/Co-Founder
www.xtremeconsulting.com

Zebra Restaurant & Wine Bar
Jim Alexander, Executive Chef/Owner
www.zebrarestaurant.net

• • •

I want to recognize the following small business support organizations and personnel I have had the pleasure to work with in my efforts to fulfill my mission of creating savvier marketers and managers in business.

**Small Business Administration –
North Carolina District Office**
Lee Cornelison, District Director
Eileen Joyce, Lead Business Development
Specialist/Marketing
Mike Ernandes, District Office Public
Information Officer
www.sba.gov

**Catawba Valley Community College –
Small Business Center**
Workforce Development Innovation
Center
Bonnie Sweeting
www.cvcc.edu

**Central Piedmont Community
College –Small Business Center**
Institute for Entrepreneurship
Rene Hode
www.cpcc.edu

**Gaston College – Small Business
Center**
Cynthia Cash
Brad Rivers
www.gaston.edu

**The Nussbaum Center for
Entrepreneurship**
University of North Carolina at
Greensboro
Cathy Daniels-Lee
www.nussbaumcfe.com

**Rowan-Cabarrus Community College
-Small Business Center**
Barbara Hall
Alesia Burris
Maggi Braun
www.rowancabarrus.edu

**Small Business and Technology
Development Center**
University of North Carolina at Charlotte
George McAllister
http://www.sbtdc.org

**Stanly Community College -Small
Business Center**
Kathy Almond
www.stanly.edu

BEFCOR
A Certified Development Company
Richard Bargoil, Director
www.befcor.com

Self-Help Charlotte NC Region
A Certified Development Company
Dale Harrold, Director
www.self-help.org

•   •   •

I would like to extend my special thanks to the following individuals. They have been my supporters, inspirations, friends, advisors, confidantes, and cheerleaders in the creation of this book and building my business. They are valued in my life and through the various stages of fulfilling my mission to help business owners become savvier marketers and managers:

Terry Ainsworth
Patsy Black
Pamela Boileau
Kelly Borth
Courtney Boone
Maggi Braun
Mary Bruce
Sharon Bunting
Marta Carlson
Pat Coffey
Gina Columna
Cindra and Steven Cowen
Kalen Cowen
Amaria DeMao
Cassandra DeMao

Savannah DeMao
Mary Ellen Ezarsky
Chastity Forester
Barbara Green
Barbara Hall
Brittany Harrigan
Ariel Hooper
Jan King
Amanda Merchant
Elizabeth Miller
Ben Palmer
Dean Palmer
Debbie Peterson
Jenny Pippin
Rosemarie & Steve Printz

Stephanie Purk
Nancy Simmons
Tamara & Russ Strupp
Monica Smiley
Kristina Smith
Wesley Stearns
Janet Sumney
Bonnie Sweeting
Sandy Washburn
Dave Yochum
Tracy Yochum
Deborah Young

•   •   •

The following resources were used for specific statistical information provided in the book.

Arbor Networks, Internet Use Analysis (8/2009)

BIA/Kelsey Study (3/2010)

CRISP Principle Study, SLD Unlimited Marketing/PR, Inc. (2004)

comsScore-TMPDM (7/2009)

"Generations Online in 2009," by Sydney Jones, Research Assistant and Susannah Fox, Associate Director, Pew Internet & American Life Project, January 28, 2009

Internet World Stats, Internet Usage and World Population Statistics (12/2009)

PaloAlto Networks, Application Usage & Risk Report (2009)

Webtrends, Inc. (2009)

Index

Breinigsville, PA USA
06 July 2010
241237BV00001BA/1/P